A Son's Journey

TAKING CARE OF MOM AND DAD

Stories, Lessons and Resources in Caring for Loved Ones

Kurt Kazanowski

First edition: July 2015
Cover design: Al Baiocchi, FrontPage Interactive
Printed in the United States of America

ISBN: 9781512384444
ISBN: 1512384445

Acknowledgements

The inspiration for this book came from my parents Helen and Conrad. Their love and dedication to raising my brother Garrett and I resulted in our ability to provide them the love and care in return, as we became their caregivers. The cycle of life.

I wouldn't have been able to write this book if it weren't for all the lessons that the thousands of families and clients we cared for through *Homewatch CareGivers* taught me and my staff. These families and clients truly are the heroes, as their challenges and life experiences help contribute to the content in this book.

To my *Homewatch CareGivers* staff, Tiffany Hoffman, Stephanie Clum, Tressa Anderson, Koreen Daniels and Ava Frakes, and the hundreds of caregivers, thank you for the tremendous amount of support you've unknowingly given me. I know I can be a pain at times!

Several key close friends and colleagues supported me in the writing of this book and I wish to acknowledge them. Thank you Joan Blackley, Debra Geihsler, Angela Colarusso, Al Baiocchi, Caryn Stumpfl and my brother Garrett. And to all my friends at La Casa Cigar Club: Thank you for your understanding as I spent most of my time writing this book at our club as opposed to participating in the comradery that binds us together. This was truly a group effort.

*Dedicated to my loving mother and father
and the best brother in the world …*

Table of Contents

Introduction

Never in my wildest dreams did I anticipate how stressful the aging and subsequent deaths of my parents, Conrad and Helen, would be. I thought being a nurse and healthcare professional would make it easier. It didn't. The same thing goes for my brother Garrett, a respiratory therapist. We simply didn't comprehend the physical, emotional and financial tolls of caring for our parents. Neither did we know where to look for help and support. I figured if my brother and I, both of us in healthcare, had a hard time dealing with all these challenges, how were other people dealing with the myriad issues of home-health and end-of-life care? The feelings of helplessness and the loss of control in trying to care for an aging loved one was not something we had thought about prior to our parents falling ill. Yet, that's one of the main reasons I'm writing this book. I don't want anyone going through what my family and I went through.

My mother and father were 10 years apart in age. As I look back on this, that age difference was a blessing. We didn't have to deal with two parents going through the same phases of aging and related illnesses at the same time. My father had a stroke at age 78. One of the first lessons I learned the hard way was how challenging, emotionally draining and difficult it is to be both a caregiver and loved one at the same time.

In retrospect, my father's journey home from the hospital and rehab unit after his stroke was one of the most stressful periods for me, my brother and mother. We were ill-prepared in every sense of the word.

The hospital sent him home with a hope and a prayer. Believe me when I tell you hope is *not* a strategy. After two months of trying to care for Dad ourselves at home, my family had to make the most emotionally draining decision of our lives to place him in a nursing home.

I felt tremendously guilty not only because of what was happening to my dad but also because of what I was thinking: Why is all this happening to me? I knew this was a selfish sentiment but I couldn't help it. While I recognized this was normal behavior and had seen many of my patients' families go through it, it still affected me a great deal.

Looking back, if the hospital had given us referrals for a personal care home health company, we most likely would have been able to keep Dad at home. He would have been much more comfortable in his own home. Mom would have been happier maintaining her daily routines in a secure environment, and we all would have been able to focus on being a family as opposed to caregivers. The silver lining to this experience is that it led me to open a personal care home health company called *Homewatch CareGivers*. Since I opened *Homewatch* in 2005, I have been able to help thousands of families avoid going through what I went through.

Five years after my father died, my brother talked Mom into moving into his home. At this point, she was just starting to experience the effects of aging. Our biggest concern at the time was the risk of her falling when she was alone. During the last few years of my mother's life, my brother and I were able to care for her better, having learned a great deal from our father's experience. I also was able to assist with her care by providing a caregiver from my company, *Homewatch*, to help out. This helped prevent caregiver burnout and supported my brother, as he was Mom's primary caregiver.

My hope with this book is that by sharing some of the true stories, tragic experiences and life-changing events my family and I went through, you'll be better equipped to care for your loved ones when that time of need arises in your life.

Over the next few chapters, I'll share strategies, approaches and resources that will guide you as you take this difficult journey. I'll be honest, it isn't going to be easy and I'm not saying there won't be troubled waters ahead, but this book is a helpful guide to assist you as you deal with *your* aging parents or loved ones.

Learning how to talk to your parents about their wishes is an art unto itself. While covering this topic, I'll share specific approaches and phraseology that will help you relate to your loved ones with compassion, respect and love, in a manner that allows them to maintain their dignity.

I'll give you some insight in recognizing the signs of caregiver burnout and how to manage them. Caregiver burnout that goes unchecked can be more damaging to this process than you could know.

I'll also give you specific criteria to follow on how to locate and hire a reliable and qualified personal care home health company.

You've probably heard many horror stories about families who have made big mistakes with their loved ones. I dedicate one chapter to how falls are one of the biggest killers of seniors and how to prevent them.

Finally, I will discuss the gift of hospice care and how families can get the support they need when a loved one faces the end of life.

CHAPTER 1

The Difficulties of Being a Caregiver *and* Loved One at the Same Time

Dad's Stroke

I was driving home from a Detroit Pistons basketball game in November 1994, when my mobile phone went off and I heard my mother's voice saying, "Dad had a stroke." My life changed forever at that moment. This started a 20-year journey for my brother and me as we dealt with my father trying to recover from his stroke, while being cognizant and respectful of Mom as she aged. Our journey was filled with many unknowns, lots of tears and, most of all, genuine love, as we cared for our parents.

As I drove home that cold November night, flashback memories of my father, mother and brother filled my thoughts. I grew up on the west side of Detroit, where I went to Redford High School. I received my bachelor's degree in Nursing from Mercy College in Detroit. I came from your typical middle-class family. Mom was a school teacher and Dad worked at Detroit Receiving Hospital in the shipping and receiving area.

My early years truly formed my life in healthcare but I didn't know it at the time. I remember at age 12 visiting my Uncle Peter, who was a pathologist at Alpena General Hospital in Alpena, Michigan. I spent time with him at the hospital and was amazed at how a hospital worked. One summer, while visiting my uncle, he had to perform an emergency autopsy late on a Saturday evening. My uncle enlisted the help of my father and me to get the body out of the freezer onto the autopsy table. That was the first time in my life I saw a body and actually assisted in a small portion of the autopsy. Instead of being squeamish or repulsed, I was fascinated by the whole process.

My Aunt Frieda was a public health nurse for the Oakland County Health Department. I remember enjoying her stories of how she would help people in their homes with health challenges and issues. I did not know it at the time, but 12 years later, I would also become a public health nurse and work for the Oakland County Health Department. Yes, life is interesting and you never know how it's going to turn out.

As a young man, I thought my professional journey would lead me to being in the restaurant business. I was 16 when I started bussing tables at a restaurant named for and owned by a Greek family named Ginopolis. I was a busboy for two years, and then, when I turned 18, I was promoted to bartender. These experiences, while different than working in the healthcare world, taught me invaluable lessons on how to interact and work with people.

From bussing tables to tending bar at Ginopolis, I learned a great deal about life and the value of a strong work ethic, all because owners Johnny and Peter Ginopolis gave me the opportunity and believed in me. My experiences also helped me appreciate the value of listening to others who needed an ear. As a result of this, I learned more about myself. I believe everyone should tend bar for a year, as it opens your eyes to the world around you and the plight of the human experience.

Instead of going into the restaurant business, however, I went to nursing school. Quite a difference in career paths, I know. There was a reason for this life-altering decision that I didn't realize until much later in life and, thankfully, it all worked out for the best. I still may have a restaurant in my future though! Over the years, I have had several opportunities to participate in restaurant ventures. I'm just waiting for the right opportunity to present itself.

I actually started my first year of college before I graduated from high school. I was part of one of those in-between-year January graduation groups. Mercy College was a nice, small Catholic college in Detroit. It was a 15-minute drive from where I lived with my parents and another five minutes to where I worked at Ginopolis.

Life was good.

I enjoyed nursing school and was the only guy in a class of 98 women. As I said, life was *good*.

In my sophomore year, I fell in love with a lovely and caring Greek woman named Lana, who also was in the nursing program. We started dating seriously and were engaged a year later. I married Lana in 1976 – the year we graduated.

We both worked together as public health nurses for the Oakland County Health Department. As I look back, I realize that this was one of the best jobs I ever had. I was able to draw on everything I learned in nursing school and more. Again, I didn't know how invaluable my experiences in the restaurant business would translate to making me a better nurse. I worked with a team of six other public health nurses, and together we served the community of Royal Oak, Michigan.

My caseload included four elementary schools, where I served as school nurse. I also worked directly with 25 or so families. Being able to work in the community and local schools to improve people's health status was exciting for me. These early experiences not only set my career path in healthcare but were filled with joy!

These eclectic life experiences helped make me who I am today. The life lessons I learned and success I achieved during my Ginopolis years, as well as being the only man in a nursing program and in my practice as a public health nurse, not only shaped my young professional life, it gave me a much-needed boost of self-confidence.

My life and career continued to evolve. I went back to school in 1980 and received a master's degree in Healthcare Administration from Wayne State University. I also pursued and achieved my Master's in Business Administration at Grand Valley State University near Grand Rapids, Michigan.

Throughout the 1980s and '90s, I worked in several hospitals and used my community-based experiences as a public health nurse to help health systems develop more community-based approaches to healthcare. These experiences prepared me for a career in home care and hospice, coming full circle back to my days as a public health nurse.

Fast forward to 1994. I was 42, married and enjoying a successful career as a hospital executive when Dad had his stroke.

Impaired on the left side of his body, Dad needed help with all aspects of personal care and activities of daily living. He was a real trooper as he went to rehab in the hospital trying to get his strength back. We never gave up the belief in our plan of bringing him home.

Watching him struggle to learn to walk with assistance and trying to communicate upset me and made me cry. The feeling of helplessness on my part must have been only a fraction of the feelings of despair and helplessness my dad felt. I spent years working in healthcare, from nursing school right up to that moment he had his stroke, and suddenly I saw hospitals in a totally different light, as a family member of a patient.

I remember feeling scared and powerless at the family meeting in the hospital before Dad was discharged. I was filled with questions but had no good answers. How was my mother going to take care of him? What would we do if we couldn't care for Dad at home? How much time would it take away from my job to help them? Dealing with the unknown about what would happen when he got home caused me many sleepless nights. I was hoping my education and practical experience as a nurse would help me get through this.

Unfortunately, I was wrong.

I actually started to experience caregiver burnout before my father got home! While my brother lived 15 minutes away from Mom and Dad, I was over an hour away. The burden for most of the planning and initial care for Dad fell to my brother.

As the days grew closer for Dad to come home, all of our anxiety levels increased. The family meeting at the hospital created more stress, as opposed to a sense of security that all would be OK as it was intended. We prepared for my dad's return home by moving his bed to the living room, because we knew he couldn't go up and down stairs any longer. Setting up a bedside commode and bed stand was something we never imagined we'd need to do. The living room quickly started to look more like a hospital room.

While the hospital helped us get the necessary equipment into the house to care for him, they didn't make any recommendations for caregivers to help us care for my dad. This left all the care, day and night, up to us.

As I look back, this was a gigantic mistake on the hospital's part. What we needed was much more emotional and social support and other assistance. While it was great the hospital helped out with the needed medical equipment, what my mother really could have used was coaching and realistic advice on what to expect when Dad got home.

It would have been helpful if the hospital social worker could have made us aware of some social support groups in the community. I should have known better, being a nurse who worked in the complex health systems. I became angry and upset with this seeming lack of support. I guess when the patient is your father, you're a son first and not a nurse. When the day came for Dad's discharge home, we were all on pins and needles and my mother was a mess. My mother's greatest worries were actually realized when she discovered she was unable to take care of my father. This broke her heart and was one of the most painful experiences for me to observe.

It became apparent from day one we were in trouble.

There was no way my petite mother, at 5 feet 2 inches and 110 pounds, could care for my dad. Dad stood 5 feet 10 inches tall and weighed 180 pounds. After his stroke, he was dead weight. Even with training on how to help lift him, my mother just couldn't do it.

My brother and I took turns going over to help – mostly my brother because of the distance. We helped with personal care and getting him up and about. You should have seen me trying to shave my dad! As I cared for him, I flashed back to better days and then started resenting the loss of those days. My feelings ranged from confidence that we could make this work and keep him at home, to dread and despair that it would kill my mother to place my father in a nursing home.

Signs and Symptoms of Caregiver Burnout

I remember learning a great deal about caregiver burnout in nursing school: what to look for, how to address it and, as a health care professional, how to assist families in dealing with burnout. I never thought, however, it would hit home and impact my life the way it did. While I was aware of the incidence of caregiver burnout, I was completely unprepared.

As the days went by, my mother, brother and I were starting to experience different degrees of burnout. Surprisingly it didn't take long! I recognized right from the beginning that it was extremely difficult to be both a son and caregiver at the same time. I guess that's why doctors don't treat their own family members.

In a nutshell, caregiver burnout is a state of physical, emotional and mental exhaustion that may be accompanied by a change in attitude about the patient – from positive and caring to negative and unconcerned. Burnout can occur when caregivers don't get the help they need, or if they try to do more than they are able – either physically or financially. Caregivers who are "burned out" may experience fatigue, stress, anxiety and depression. Many caregivers also feel guilty if they spend time on themselves, rather than on their ill or elderly loved ones.

The symptoms of caregiver burnout are similar to the symptoms of stress and depression. They include:

- Withdrawal from friends, family and other loved ones;
- Loss of interest in activities previously enjoyed;
- Feeling blue, irritable, hopeless and helpless;
- Changes in appetite, weight or both;
- Changes in sleep patterns;
- Getting sick more often;
- Feelings of wanting to hurt yourself or the person for whom you are caring;
- Emotional and physical exhaustion; and
- Irritability.

As I look back on all this, I became even angrier at the hospital that didn't help us find a personal care home health company. As I said previously, this was the major driving force in me starting *Homewatch CareGivers*, and in writing this book.

One thing I have noticed in my work as the owner of *Homewatch CareGivers* is how a medical crisis can tear a family apart. Thank goodness this wasn't an issue for my family.

Yet, caregiver burnout can bring out the worst in everyone. I have seen so many families fight over how they believe their loved one should be cared for, and especially about how to allocate the finances that need to go into caring for a loved one. Family members start arguing about whom should be doing what or whom is doing more, while craving affirmation for their roles. While all this is going on, their loved one's care and necessities go out the window! The family tension continues to escalate and the signs and symptoms of caregiver burnout begin to show up.

There were actually several reasons I wrote this book. One of my objectives in writing was to not only share my experiences but to also give helpful hints that will hopefully make your experiences less stressful and much more positive.

The other is to help empower families to be more in control and know what to ask about when dealing with a loved one with a challenging health condition, as you bring them back home to live.

The following are some of the signs of caregiver burnout my family and I started to experience, with some helpful hints on how to deal with them:

1. **I felt furious one minute; sad and helpless the next.** No matter what you call it, second-hand stress or caregiver burnout, I had it! I was feeling a disparaging mix of physical and emotional exhaustion. As I rode the emotional rollercoaster of caregiving, I became easily overwhelmed and angry. I lost my appetite and didn't eat. I was exhausted even after a full night's sleep. My brain was foggy and I no longer cared about the things that used to bring me joy.

   My life had changed in profound ways, so it was natural to feel frustrated and to grieve for what I had lost. Intellectually I knew that untreated anxiety or depression could be serious and that if I didn't take good care of myself, I couldn't care for my dad and help my family, but I still had trouble managing my feelings and this overload of emotions.

   Recommended fix: If you experience similar feelings and think you may have caregiver burnout, consider these suggestions: First, check in with your doctor to rule out any medical conditions that can trigger symptoms of mental health problems. Let your doctor know that you are a caregiver and might need support to be able to continue in this role. Finally, remind yourself that while you are doing everything you can, you will never be able to do everything – and that's OK, too.

2. **I caught every bug that came my way.** As a nurse, I know stress doesn't just make you anxious and depressed; it takes a toll on your body. I was getting so run down that my immune system was not only more susceptible to germs and infection, I also was getting sick more often and staying sick longer. My body definitely was trying to tell me something.

   Recommended fix: Don't let routine checkups slide because you don't think you have the time. See your primary care doctor and your dentist regularly. Ditto for immunizations, mammograms and other recommended screenings. Eating a nutritious diet and getting at least seven hours of sleep a night boosts your body's natural defenses.

3. **I was snapping at everyone.** When you feel helpless and overwhelmed, you're more likely to overreact to little things people do or don't do. That was me! I was rude and argumentative (a real pain in the ass!) to people closest to me. Thank goodness my close friends knew what I was going through. Just like a toddler having a tantrum, you need a timeout to adjust your attitude.

   Recommended fix: Don't set the bar so high that you can never meet it. Practice taking deep breaths, in through your nose and out through your mouth, until you get yourself calm and in control. Pick up the phone and make a call to a friend. I was pretty good at doing that. Studies show that simply giving voice to your frustrations and fears dials down tension and eases the isolation that shadows caregivers. We all like to be in control. Mapping out a daily routine that you try to stick to will also give you a greater sense of control. Prioritize your to-do list, whether it's grocery shopping or taking Mom to a doctor's appointment. Don't worry about things lower down on your list that just don't get done. Tomorrow is another day.

4. **I knew I should exercise, but just didn't take the time.** Not having time to work out is a sure sign of caregiver burnout. No one functions well in crisis mode day after day.

   Recommended fix: Force yourself to get moving. Exercise is the best stress reliever. Not only will you feel better right away, the surge of endorphins that exercise triggers lifts your mood, clears your head and helps you sleep better at night. A brisk 30-minute walk or jog on the treadmill, even a 10-minute walk around the block, jumpstarts your brain, soothes nerves and powers up your immune system.

5. **I couldn't recall the last time I met a friend for dinner.** Everyone needs a break from time to time. I found that my motivation to help my dad, which was driven by a mix of love, loyalty and a dash of guilt, prevented me from seeing my friends. Thankfully, my good friends took the initiative to make plans with me.

   Recommended fix: I'm not suggesting a two-week trip to Jamaica, though that would be excellent, right? An overnight visit with your spouse to a cozy bed and breakfast, a night out with a friend or even a few hours at your favorite coffee shop with a book or taking in a movie can be restorative. One stipulation: Taking a break doesn't mean doing something for a friend or running errands.

6. **My brother was the go-to caregiver. Always.** My brother Garrett had the hardest job. Because he lived closest to my parents, he was always the "go-to" caregiver for my dad. Try going it alone and you'll quickly hit bottom. Garrett got close.

   Recommended fix: The following are some excellent ideas for all of you go-to caregivers:

   - Establish a network of relatives, friends or people in the community you can call on.
   - Schedule a family meeting or video chat about who does what and who pays for it.
   - Let everyone know you will not be available to host holiday meals, organize the church book drive or any other draining activities that you may have normally handled.
   - Keep a to-do list with you and whip it out when others ask if they can help. Your neighbor might be happy to spend a few hours at your house while you go to the gym. A friend can buy groceries when they are at the store.

Homewatch CareGivers –
My Contribution to You

There *was* a silver lining to my family's tragic experiences. What I learned the hard way was something I never want another family to go through.

Years after my father died, I had the opportunity to open a personal care home health company called *Homewatch CareGivers*. A good friend of mine, Debra Geihsler, partnered with me to start *Homewatch CareGivers*, a franchise model that we bought into. *Homewatch* (**www.thehomecareexpert.com**) is a leader in providing in-home personal care services. The main reason I selected *Homewatch* over all the other franchises out there was their commitment to helping me be successful by providing training materials and support on hiring caregivers.

At the end of the day, it's all about the quality of the caregiver we place in a family's home and creating the best experience for the patients we care for and their families. *Homewatch CareGivers* is committed to the relentless pursuit of caregiver excellence.

From day one, I promised myself that I would try my best to help people NOT go through the same experiences I did with my dad. *Homewatch* gave me the chance to help thousands of families through this deeply emotional and trying time. I'll discuss more about *Homewatch* later, but first, let me explain exactly what a personal care home health company does.

Keeping Patients Safe in Their Homes

There are actually two types of home care companies: skilled home health-care and personal care home health companies. A skilled home healthcare company provides restorative sets of services provided by nurses, physical therapists, occupational therapists, speech therapists and home health aides. For patients that qualify, these services are often covered and paid for by Medicare, Medicaid or private insurance companies. Typically patients receive skilled home care services when they get out of the hospital if they require care to help regain strength and/or the ability to perform activities of daily living. Services are provided at home. Nurses or therapists usually see patients at home a few days a week for a period of a few months.

A personal care home health company like *Homewatch CareGivers* is a non-medical company that provides a set of services ranging from companionship and transportation up to 24-hour, live-in care. At *Homewatch*, we customize our approach for each family, with no request being too small or large. Our clients need support to help keep them safe, secure and independent in their homes – whether that's an apartment, a house or even an assisted living community. Here are a few examples of how *Homewatch* helps families care for loved ones, enabling the patients to maintain their dignity while preventing caregiver burnout:

- Our caregivers support the home and family by providing light housekeeping and maintenance, doing laundry and preparing nutritious meals.
- Our caregivers can provide safe transportation and run errands, helping patients maintain a sense of independence by driving them to the store or out for social events, church and get-togethers with friends. Keeping up a social network can help fight loneliness and stave off depression in patients.
- Companionship can come in many forms. By simply being at the home, our friendly caregivers can keep an eye on loved ones during the day or at night, assuring their safety. Playing cards or board games can help a loved one stay mentally sharp.

- Caregivers also can provide personal care services, such as giving showers or baths, getting patients dressed, serving meals and helping patients eat, taking patients out for walks, reminding them to take their medications or driving them to medical appointments.

Who Can Benefit from Personal Care Home Health Services?

Patients living with Alzheimer's disease or Dementia and their families can benefit greatly from having a personal care home health company assist them. In addition, families with loved ones who have suffered strokes or traumatic brain injury and other complex conditions can benefit, particularly after discharge from a hospital or rehab unit. The first few days home can be challenging. *Homewatch* assists with "reentry" and helps establish positive routines, while limiting potential hazards in the home. *Homewatch* also provides extra support to folks in assisted living communities.

One of the things I love most about being the owner of *Homewatch CareGivers* is the ability to touch people's lives and help them avoid the things I am writing about in this book. In the following passage, I'll tell you about a couple I worked closely with and how *Homewatch* helped make a difference in their lives. Their names were changed to protect their privacy but the story is true.

Helping the Smiths Maintain Their Independence

I have a passion for speaking and presenting my story to groups and audiences around the world. I met Mrs. Ruth Smith at one of those events. This time, it was a local Rotary Club meeting. I was telling the Rotary Club about my personal experience with my dad and my caregiver burnout. I talked about how difficult it was to be a loved one and caregiver at the same time. As I was talking, I noticed a woman in the back nodding her head in agreement. After my talk, the woman approached me and told me she was experiencing all the signs of caregiver burnout I mentioned.

Mrs. Smith was a woman in her late 60s. She had a husband at home who was diagnosed five years earlier with Parkinson's disease. Parkinson's disease is a progressive disorder of the nervous system that affects movement. Mrs. Smith said that her husband's condition developed gradually and started with a barely noticeable tremor in just one hand. But while Mr. Smith's tremor grew steadily, his disorder also caused stiffness and slowing of his movements. His speech became soft and slurred and his face, which previously showed expression, became expressionless.

During the past year, Mrs. Smith explained, Mr. Smith's condition deteriorated to the point where Mrs. Smith had to help her husband with direct personal care. She needed to assist him with dressing himself. She made sure he was safely able to maneuver the stairs. She also needed to support him with some other activities of daily living. As Mrs. Smith told me her story, she started to cry. I made an appointment with her immediately to visit the Smiths at home the next day to complete an assessment and design a plan of care.

John Smith had just turned 81 and was a proud man. He was a very successful attorney before he retired. I could tell as we spoke, by Mr. Smith's acknowledgement of his situation, that he needed extra help. He understood that his disease was worsening and he was losing his independence. At the end of my time with the family that first day, Mr. Smith caught me alone and said, "I know I could use a little extra help, but I really want a caregiver, so my wife can have her life back." My eyes swelled up as I could feel the love Mr. Smith had for his wife. As I said previously, a caregiver can help the entire family – not just the patient!

I completed the assessment, including a fall risk evaluation, the needed paperwork to start care, which the Smiths wanted to begin the next week, and a Care Plan. A Care Plan is a written plan of care we use at *Homewatch* to refine the family's wishes. We create and share a draft of the Care Plan with the family, so they know exactly what they can expect from our caregivers. An example of Mr. Smith's Care Plan can be seen at the end of this chapter. The goals of the Care Plan we created together were:

1. To help Mr. Smith begin each day safely and help with his personal care needs;
2. To be a good companion to Mr. Smith; and
3. To give Mrs. Smith four hours per day to lead her life and alleviate her caregiver burnout.

The Care Plan looked like this: The caregiver would arrive at the house at 7 a.m. each day and help Mr. Smith get out of bed and up and going. After helping Mr. Smith with a shower and getting dressed, the caregiver would fix breakfast. Mrs. Smith would head out to meet a friend for coffee or to do some shopping. Mr. Smith could feed himself, so as he was eating breakfast, the caregiver would start a load of laundry and clean Mr. Smith's bedroom and bathroom. After breakfast, the caregiver would help Mr. Smith with his daily exercise. Mr. Smith had a special DVD of exercises that were created for him by his neurologist. The caregiver was there to support and be Mr. Smith's personal coach, giving him encouragement as he worked out and to ensure his safety and prevent him from falling. The rest of the morning, Mr. Smith would relax and the caregiver would complete household chores. At noon, Mrs. Smith would come home and the caregiver would leave. Every once in a while, Mrs. Smith would schedule the caregiver to stay the full day if she was going to be out.

Balance, a sense of calm and peace of mind were restored to the Smith household. The Smiths loved each other and saw the caregiver as a gift to both of them. The caregiver helped maintain Mr. Smith's sense of independence, and Mr. Smith could see his wife was much happier and confident that he was safe and secure when she was away from home.

You may be wondering what this kind of care cost the Smiths. The fee was $21.25 per hour. The caregiver was there 35 hours per week. So the weekly cost was $743.75 or $2,975 per month. We were able to help the Smiths access Mr. Smith's Veteran's Affairs (VA) benefits for Aid and Attendance, which helped off-set the expense in the amount of $1,200 each month.

In-home personal care can be expensive. The best advice I can give here is to seek the advice of a certified financial planner or other financial expert, who can help you plan for and offer suggestions and strategies to cover this type of care, such as the following four methods:

1. A family can pay with its own personal funds. Most people draw upon their savings and investments. When a family is involved, many times the children will share the financial challenges of caring for a parent.

2. Veterans may quality for the VA benefit called Aid and Attendance. A surviving spouse also qualifies for this benefit. The VA has advocates who can help a family complete the application, submit it and keep an eye on the application's progress.

3. Long-term-care insurance can be a source of payment as well. If you have such a policy, you can negotiate with the insurance company to pay for personal home care. An insurance company may gladly pay for the less-expensive option of personal home care over a skilled nursing home facility.

4. A reverse mortgage, which allows money to be drawn from your home to pay for expenses, is another option. The main drawback is that at the end of the draw period, you will no longer own your home.

In addition to a financial planner, I urge you to seek the counsel of an elder law attorney. These professionals can help you navigate the financial and legal options available and help you make an informed decision.

Watching Mom Age

After two months of trying to care for Dad at home, we made the most difficult decision of our collective lives and placed him in a nursing home. It was a skilled nursing facility close to where Mom lived. We didn't have anyone to give us the advice outlined above, so we felt we had no option but to place Dad in a facility. Three months later, my father died. I believe Dad realized he would never be the same and have the capacity to love my mother and his family the way he wanted and he just gave up on life.

I remember the last time I saw Dad alive. He was declining quickly. He looked weak and lost. As I was with him, he was grabbing at things in front of him that weren't there. It is a normal sign that someone is close to death. I climbed up into bed with him and just held him and cried. I felt so close to him and I think of this moment every day of my life. He died two days later.

My father's death was a big loss yet also a big relief. While caring for Dad at home was stressful, seeing him in a nursing home broke my heart and made me angry. I was angry at how unprepared I was for what happened. I was angry at myself for all the feelings I experienced. I was VERY angry at the hospital and how they provided NO support in helping my family deal with bringing Dad home. After his passing, it was like coming out of the abyss.

After my dad's funeral, my brother and I noticed Mom looked much older than before Dad's stroke just a few months earlier. It was amazing how the stress and ordeal of seeing Dad die aged my mother. I remember discussing with my brother how long Mom would be able to stay safe and secure living alone. It turned out to be about five years.

Over the next few years, we were good sons and helped Mom enjoy life as best as we could. In the back of our minds, however, we wondered if we would have to deal with another situation like our dad's. Although Mom lived alone at home, she did very well for a time. Mom lived in a co-op living community with great neighbors and friends that helped out. My brother and I stopped by often. I ended up moving to Plymouth, where my mother lived, and was able to stop over and have breakfast with her most mornings as I headed to work. I enjoyed my special "alone" time with Mom and I felt better knowing she was doing well.

The biggest fear my brother and I had was Mom falling down the stairs. She lived in a two-story house and her bedroom was upstairs. We both knew that breaking a hip would most likely be the beginning of the end. As my mom aged, the first change we noticed was her gait and ability to walk. She had a touch of scoliosis (curvature) of the spine, which made it more difficult for her to stand up straight and walk. My brother worked with Mom on the best way to get up and down the stairs safely.

After five years, we were able to convince Mom to move in with my brother. This was a willing but sad time for my mother. Our greatest fear had, unfortunately, come true. My mom had suffered a few falls that, thankfully, were not major but they showed us what the future would hold if we didn't act promptly.

Here I am with my beautiful mother, Helen, and wonderful brother, Garrett, in happier times.

Even at my brother's house, Mom lived fairly independently. Staying with my brother allowed her to maintain that independence, while we were able to support her as she aged at home. We also were able to keep a loving eye on her.

Mom lived safely with my brother for several years. Then one day, while my brother was at work, Mom went outside to get the newspaper and fell directly on her face and right arm. Her face was so swollen and bruised, it looked like she went 10 rounds with Mike Tyson! The good news was she did not break any bones.

At that point, we convinced Mom it was time to have a caregiver from *Homewatch* come into the house when my brother was at work. The journey with my mom had just taken a significant turn. I will talk about this experience in a later chapter, so keep reading to see how it all worked out.

The following is the actual Care Plan my company, *Homewatch Caregivers*, created for the Smith family I mentioned earlier.

Homewatch Caregivers: Care Plan for John and Ruth Smith
Oct. 16, 2014

Source of Referral: Caring.Com and a friend
Client's Address: XX Northville Lane, Northville, MI 48167
Client's Phone Number(s): 248-XXX-XXXX

Services Requested: Ruth Smith is seeking support in caring for her husband, John, who has Parkinson's disease. Her current request is for companionship and safety support services when Mrs. Smith is away from the home. There are a handful of days per month that Mrs. Smith has standing appointments and expects to be away from the house. Mrs. Smith also may have situations when she calls the office for a caregiver to come over to the house when she needs to leave suddenly or if something comes up outside of her usual schedule. The initial schedule starts as follows:

> ➢ Wednesday, Oct. 29: 11:30 a.m. to 4 p.m.
> ➢ Monday, Nov. 3: 5:30 p.m. to 9:30 p.m.
> ➢ Monday, Nov. 17: 5 p.m. to 8:30 p.m.
> ➢ Saturday, Dec. 6: 5 p.m. to 9 p.m.

We will establish a regular schedule with the family after the new year.

Price: $21.25/hr. This case will start a companionship case and no personal care is required at this time. Mrs. Smith would like an invoice emailed to her and to have her credit card charged.

Situation: Mr. John Smith is an 81-year-old gentleman who was diagnosed with Parkinson's disease five years ago. Mr. Smith is independent in his activities of daily living. He sometimes has difficulty verbally expressing himself. The major focus of the Care Plan is safety and fall prevention. Mrs. Smith reached out to Homewatch to provide support for her husband when she is away from the home. Mr. Smith is a retired attorney whose office was located in downtown Plymouth. The family lives in Northville. They have been in this home for 35 years. The house has two stories with two living areas downstairs where John enjoys spending time. The bedrooms are upstairs. Mr. Smith requires support for fall prevention when going up and down the stairs. The caregiver MUST grab Mr. Smith's belt loop in the back when coming down the stairs. Mr. Smith is on an exercise program and may benefit from support from the caregiver. At a recent physician appointment, it was noted that Mr. Smith's balance had declined and is becoming an issue. The caregiver also will assist Mrs. Smith by relieving her from her caregiver responsibility and allow her to be a loved one. Mr. Smith's appetite is good. He just needs assistance in setting up his meals at the dinner table.

Caregiver responsibility: Following is the initial list of activities that will comprise the Care Plan and caregiver tasks:

1. Safety is the major focus of the Care Plan and the caregiver's main responsibility. This includes being with Mr. Smith when he is going up and down stairs and supporting ambulation at all times in the home to prevent falls.
2. The caregiver should stand by as Mr. Smith takes a shower for safety and any support needed.
3. The caregiver will provide meal preparation (if requested) based on what the client would like. If the meal is ready, the caregiver will set the dinner table and help Mr. Smith get to the dinner table to eat.
4. The caregiver will clean the kitchen after meals and straighten up as needed to maintain a safe environment.
5. The caregiver will do laundry as requested.
6. The caregiver will vacuum and clean the house as requested.
7. The caregiver will run errands as requested (e.g. picking up medications, driving Mr. Smith to medical appointments, shopping, going on "munchies" runs, etc.).
8. The caregiver will provide companionship, social interaction and mental stimulation to Mr. Smith (e.g., sitting and watching football games on TV together, playing cards, etc.).
9. The caregiver will remind Mr. Smith to take his medication.
10. Finally, the caregiver will support Mrs. Smith as requested.

Respectfully Submitted,

Kurt A. Kazanowski, MS, RN, CHE
734-658-6162, www.thehomecareexpert.com

CHAPTER 2

How to Talk to Your Parents

My brother Garrett and I never had to have the hard talk with our parents about giving up the keys to the car. Dad's debilitating stroke and rapid decline until the day he died a few months later kept us from having to broach this difficult topic. It was just understood his days of driving were over. And my mother, God bless her, gave up her keys on her own one day, saying it was time she not drive anymore. That was a pleasant surprise for my brother and me. This was a good thing, as one of the last times I drove with my mom, I was telling myself it was time for that talk! You should have been in the car with me. Let's just say it was a wild ride.

My mother wasn't one of those typical "old lady drivers" who go 25 in the fast lane on the highway. On the contrary, she drove like a race car driver on the Indianapolis Speedway! Now I know where I got my lead foot! I am certain that if she would have kept on driving, she would have hit something or someone one day with such a great deal of force that she would have done a lot of damage. But my brother and I never had to have that tough conversation with her, thankfully. We did, however, speak to her about getting a caregiver to come into the home when she needed some assistance. In retrospect, we should have had that talk with her much sooner. Thousands of families are faced with having these types of conversations with their elder parents. I hope this chapter will help you and your loved ones by giving you the tools to manage this type of discussion and others.

In my work, as owner of *Homewatch CareGivers*, I meet with families every day who are going through this difficult period and facing the task of talking with their parents or aging loved ones about a number of sensitive topics. These topics range from driver safety and staying safe in the home they may have lived in for 30, 40 or even 50 years, to bringing in a caregiver to help support them as they age.

It may be very tough to convince your parents about the necessity of having a stranger come into their home to provide a little extra support but it's even more challenging to discuss moving them into an assisted living community. All these subjects are recognizably difficult and stressful but necessary.

Definitely not limited to adult children and their aging parents, spouses also have to talk to each other about their inevitable aging and what plans they want and need to make to stay in their own homes as their physical and/or mental faculties begin to decline. They also need to make plans if one or both become ill and they're in need of support and assistance.

During my tenure at *Homewatch*, I remember one couple, Bob and Sue, who hired my company to come into their home to provide care only after several months of the wife trying to convince her husband to accept a caregiver in the home.

Bob was 79 years old and suffered from Multiple Sclerosis (MS), a progressive disease affecting Bob's brain and spinal cord. His early MS symptoms included weakness, tingling, numbness and blurred vision. Later, his MS caused muscle stiffness, thinking problems and urinary problems. Bob, a retired orthopedic surgeon, was a very proud man, who saw having a caregiver coming into the house as a threat to his independence and sense of control.

I made three visits to the couple's home with our nurse, Stephanie, before Bob finally agreed to "give it a try." Through our conversations and emails, I could tell Sue was in desperate need of a little extra help. I knew we could provide a solution for her situation. Her caregiver burnout was building and the caregiver we provided from *Homewatch* was needed just as much for her as for her husband. Sue was trying everything to make it Bob's idea that accepting a little extra help was OK.

This is a more common experience than you might imagine, as one person's condition is causing safety concerns for the other family members. The following is an excerpt from an email I received from Sue after Bob finally agreed to having a caregiver come into his home:

Well, you two – pat yourselves on the back. Bob liked Neon, as did I. He wanted a schedule of her dates/times and asked for her to be here longer on a couple of days. Who'd have thought? Stephanie, please advise if your Saturdays are taken for Neon.
Thanks again for all your help. We'll see how tomorrow goes.
-Sue

"The Talk"

You can avoid "the talk" with your loved ones because it's uncomfortable, or be proactive and look for an opportunity to open a positive dialogue. I have found through experience that opening a dialogue is something your parents truly need and will appreciate. Folks are more aware and sensitive to their own situations as they age and all they want is a loving and helping hand to help lead them from here to there. Keep in mind, your parents are mature adults, not children, and will appreciate your respect, candor and honest assistance. While you should be firm, you should not bully or manipulate your loved ones into doing something they simply don't want to do.

Imagining your aging parents as senior citizens seems unbelievable to some. I hear this from many of the people I work with:

"Isn't it too soon to try to talk to my parents about the future?"

"They seem to be in good health."

"What if they won't take my concerns seriously?"

Here is what I hear …

- I hope they'll stay this way forever.
- I hope they'll always be able to live on their own.
- I hope they'll always be able to drive.
- I hope they'll have enough money to keep up their lifestyle until the end.

Remember, as I said earlier, hope is *not* a plan.

Unfortunately, your parents' health and vitality will not always be a given. No matter how healthy your parents have always been, they are only one fall, one accident or one serious illness away from a crisis. Events like these lead many of my clients to call *Homewatch* with an "SOS" message. They have an urgent need for a caregiver because of a sudden change or incident. My best advice is not to wait until something happens. Be proactive! The following are some suggestions on how to start and conduct a loving and productive dialogue with your parents.

The Art of the Dialogue

One of life's most challenging moments is one we never think about until the time comes: Having the aging talk with your mom and dad. As I look back, my brother and I should have spoken to Mom a little sooner. My brother Garrett, however, did a fantastic job visiting our mom often and talking with her frequently about all sorts of things related to her future. My mother and father always gave me the room and support to learn and grow, even if I fell once in a while. I always knew they were there for me when I needed them. When they got older, it was time for me to repay the favor and be there for them. It's a funny thing how life is a circle. In many cases, we end up playing the parental role with our parents, and often, we're not prepared for it.

A great number of the *Homewatch* families we have served over the years told us they never thought about having "the talk" with their parents until one day … BAM. In many cases, folks didn't notice the subtle signs of decline in their parents until something major happened. After all, we look up to our parents as the strong family decision-makers who helped guide and mold us into who we are today. It's hard to think of them in need of help and support.

"The Talk" Can Take Its Toll On You!

It can be extremely challenging knowing when and how to start having the aging talk with your parents. I remember one time I spoke to my mother about life without Dad and my concerns for her safety as she aged and lived alone.

My mom and I discussed many important decisions over a good meal.

I reflect back to the emotional and psychological realities from that talk and wish I hadn't had to face it. Yet as adults, it's a reality many of us have to confront. The talk I had with her made me realize that she was still my mother but was no longer able to be the same person she was in her younger years. She was getting older, and, all of a sudden it hit me that *I* was aging, too. I really wasn't that far away from where Mom was at that particularly difficult moment in time.

One of the biggest challenges often ends up being the process of stripping away our parents' independence. As we think about what all this entails, it can be very daunting. For instance, if they drive, we may have to take away their keys and make provisions for them to get around either by public transportation or caregivers. This often makes them feel like a dependent child that has to ask permission for basic things, such as coming and going. Again, here's the cycle of life presenting itself! I've observed that this can be one of the hardest things families and elder loved ones can go through: Accepting that they can no longer do all the things they were accustomed to doing almost their entire lives because of their advancing years. Other examples of major changes we may not ever think about could be such things as restrictions on eating certain foods (for diabetics) or social limitations, such as not being able to go to church, weekly bridge club, shopping or the beauty parlor.

The major goal and mission of personal care home health companies, such as my company, *Homewatch CareGivers*, is to help people stay safe and independent in their *own* homes or wherever home may be for them at that time. Our caregivers nurture independence as opposed to dependency. By providing companionship, transportation and general overall assistance, our company helps seniors stay connected to life, their relationships and routines, while maintaining their dignity and sense of independence.

I wanted to take a minute here to provide some thoughts on how to approach your parents, so you can have the aging talk in the most loving, compassionate and effective way possible. These helpful tips can be adjusted to work for your personal situation because we all have our own special relationships and conversation styles. These eight tips will help create a positive experience and provide a good platform for the changes that will become necessary as your parent ages. I hope these tips help make your talk with your parents the best it can be.

Tips for "The Talk" With Mom and Dad

1. Start by taking a deep breath and relax yourself before each dialogue session you have with your folks. Keep this wise saying in mind: "First seek to understand, before you seek to be understood." You haven't walked in their shoes and don't really know what they're thinking or going through, so keep an open mind and really listen to them.
2. Approach your parents from a place of compassion, love and caring and not from the perspective as an expert or authority. None of us appreciates a bossy person or being told what to do. Imagine someone trying to tell you what to do and take away your freedom. Think about how your parents might be feeling. A way to open this door is to thank your parents for raising and caring for you and letting them know you want to return the favor.

3. See the glass as half-full, not half-empty. Instead of pointing out inadequacies directly, let your parents know you've noticed some things like absentmindedness, hearing loss, being a little unsteady on their feet, etc. and you would like to help. Offering a plan or strategy can help you show your parents you care about their needs. For example, tell your Mom you made an appointment with the hearing specialist and you'll go with her. Suggest that the doctor can make her life easier by correcting the situation. Remind your mom how much she loved to engage in conversation and debate with others when her hearing was more acute – and suggest that maybe a hearing aid can help. You can do this with almost any situation you are attempting to assist your parents with.

4. Practice, practice and practice again. Role-playing with your spouse or a friend is a good way to help you feel more comfortable before you speak to your parents.

5. When you believe it's time for them to get a caregiver, make sure you give them the ability to choose that person and allow them to be actively involved in the process. Help them feel as if they still have control over their own lives. Remember Bob and Sue: Sue's strategy of involving her husband in the selection of the caregiver helped Bob perceive that the caregiver was his own decision, which ultimately made things much easier.

6. It's all in the presentation. The trick here is to allow them to realize their needs and be able to express an opinion. For example, ask your parents how they feel about their living situation. Is the house becoming more difficult to keep up than normal? How do they feel about driving or getting around town? Ask them if they still enjoy cooking at home or visiting their friends. Remember, "First seek to understand ..." When you suggest solutions to their problems, this sets you up as more of a loving and concerned son or daughter and less of a "boss" or authority figure. For example, at *Homewatch*, we counsel family members to start discussions like the following: "Mom, I've always enjoyed your delicious home-cooked dinners and remember how much you loved to cook. Now it seems like cutting up vegetables is a little difficult for you because your eyesight is not

what it used to be." Or, "Dad, I know now that standing for extended periods of time is hard for you. I can see the pain in your face. Could you use some help with the yard and garden?" When it comes time to suggest a caregiver, highlight that you'll look for a caregiver that also enjoys the same activities your parent enjoys, such as cooking. If the caregiver can assist your parents with the facets of daily life that are now a challenge, they may just go for it. You also should suggest that your parents be intimately involved when it's time to interview a possible caregiver.

7. Approach the conversation casually at first. Don't make it a formal thing. In other words, don't make an appointment to "talk." For most people, scheduling a formal discussion doesn't go down too well, whether it's your parent or anyone else. That approach almost always leads to a feeling of dread. You want to sit down and have coffee with them, and when you see your parent doing something he or she has difficulty with, you can then say, "Hey Mom, are you still enjoying that?" This will make things seem natural.

8. Physical proximity and touch often disarm a defensive situation. For example, a caring hand on your mom or dad's hand or a big hug can go a long way.

Please remember that the whole goal of having the aging talk with your parents is to make sure you end up protecting their safety, independence and health. Your kind and sensitive words will help them continue enjoying their golden years. All of us want to maintain our independence as long as we can. By approaching "the talk" out of love and compassion, you will be so much better received than if you choose to approach it from a place of control or during a stressful time.

On my *Homewatch Caregivers* website, I write a blog and post weekly about topics related to caring for aging loved ones. To check out my blog, go to **www.thehomecareexpert.com**. In the **Resource** section, the first dropdown on the menu is **Home Care Blog**. Click here. I hope you and your family find this helpful.

101 Phone Calls per Day

I was in the *Homewatch* office on a Thursday afternoon when I received a call from a woman named Mary. When I answered the phone, Mary's first words were, "When can you start services for my mother?" Mary went on to say that she lived about an hour away from her mother's home. There was a sound of desperation in Mary's voice. When I asked Mary what was going on, she replied, "I'm receiving 100 calls a day from my mom asking questions about this, that and the other thing." She shared that most of the questions were the same ones over and over again. Mary went on to say her mother lives alone, is 86 years old and is in relativity good health but her memory and cognitive abilities are starting to decline. Mary's mother, Pam, lived alone for the last 11 years since her husband passed away. She was a retired school teacher and had a small group of close friends who lived in the neighborhood. Mary went on to say that she was going over to her mother's house a few times per week. I could tell in talking with Mary she was becoming worn out and I could start to identify the signs of caregiver burnout from what she was saying.

When I asked Mary what would help, she said, "I need a caregiver to go over to Mom's house three times a week to make sure she's alright and safe." Mary also was concerned that her mother was still driving and feared she was going to get into an accident. During our conversation, she continued to express that her mother was not eating as well as she had in previous years and was no longer able to keep the house clean and organized. When I asked Mary if she had spoken to her mother about a caregiver, she replied, "No." I then inquired if her mother Pam would be receptive to receiving a little extra help from a caregiver, and again, she said, "No." This negative response told me that this was not going to be an easy task for Mary to convince her mother to accept the help she needed.

I shared with Mary that I would be more than happy to meet her over at her mother's house to get a better idea of how her mother was really feeling about her situation and assess what was going on. But first, Mary needed to talk to her mother. I coached and encouraged Mary to use some of the techniques and approaches we have been discussing here. Mary felt that these points were valid and we spent the next 45 minutes going over how Mary would have "the talk" with her mother. Mary was seeing her mother on the next Saturday, and we agreed I would call Mary on Monday to check in and see how it went.

Mary and Pam

I called Mary mid-morning on Monday, as I was eager to see how her talk with her mother went. When Mary answered the phone, I asked about their conversation. "Well, our talk was mixed. My mom did recognize she could use a little extra help but wanted *me* to provide that help." I could sense Mary was frustrated. I asked if her mother was the slightest bit receptive to the idea of taking a "test drive" with a caregiver to see how, or if, it would work. Mary stated she didn't know. We agreed to meet on Wednesday after work at her mother's home for further discussion on the idea.

On Wednesday, we met at Pam's house at 6 p.m. Pam was an elegant, petite woman who walked with the support of a cane. The house was a three-bedroom ranch with a large backyard. While the house was clean, there was "stuff" all over the place. Pam was very guarded and let it be known that she was not in favor of having a stranger come into her house to help her. Mary and I had our work cut out for us. Mary started to press her mother to accept a caregiver. I asked Mary to hold off, while I had Pam show me around her house, so I could complete an assessment with special attention to the risk of falls. I also wanted to talk with Pam alone to flush out her feelings, concerns and ideas. Pam was a joyful woman and full of energy. Her wit was sharp and I could sense she was a proud woman and wanted to maintain her independence for as long as she could. These were Pam's strong attributes. She was, however, a little fragile on her feet and unsteady at times. I found it to be somewhat difficult to navigate the house because there was an exorbitant amount of clutter all over the place. Based on what I observed, a fall was a high probability. I sat with Pam and started our dialogue with a question.

"Pam, how would you feel about having a personal helper come to your house to assist you with keeping your house in order?"

Her reply was, "What do you mean?"

"Well, I know your daughter is worried about you and I am sure we could kill two birds with one stone here."

Pam said, "How so?"

"Well," I said, "How would you like a woman to come into your house three times per week for three to four hours at a time to help you get your house and yard organized?"

"You mean she can help with my yard and garden?" I had hit a soft spot with Pam. She had a lovely yard and garden that was falling into disarray. I said to Pam, "Yes, your personal assistant could help you keep your garden up, go down in the basement to do your laundry and help you with special projects around the house."

"Really?" Pam said.

"Yes, really," I replied back. Then Pam said, "I don't want a stranger in my house." A roadblock like this is not too uncommon when talking to an elderly, independent person.

"I tell you what, Pam … how about if I bring over a personal assistant (code word for caregiver) for you to interview? Then, if you like her, you can "test drive" her for a few weeks and see how you like it."

That did the trick. Pam said, "Ok, let's try it."

"Wow," I thought to myself, "It worked!"

We let Mary know right away and she was very pleased. The following day, I brought one of my caregivers, Kathy, over to the house and she and Pam hit it off tremendously. Kathy was a mature woman in her 50s and she and Pam acted like long-lost friends.

Not unlike a matchmaking service, there is either chemistry or not with placing caregivers. Thank goodness, there was chemistry between Pam and Kathy. I am happy to report after seven months, Pam and Kathy are doing well and Mary couldn't be happier.

The 5 Don'ts When Talking with Your Parents

The following is a post from my blog about how to talk to a loved one about aging. It gives you a good idea of what *not* to say when engaged in a dialogue with your parents.

Over my career as a public health nurse and owner of *Homewatch CareGivers*, I have experienced thousands of family meetings and dialogues between senior parents and their adult children that have not always been the most productive.

Seniors often know that their memories, cognitive and physical abilities are declining, and reminders are not well received. Nobody likes to be criticized, and comments pointing out someone's shortcomings, even if they're true, can be very hurtful and insensitive. Even when we manage to hold our tongues, frustration lingers and body language speaks volumes. I've "been there, done that" with my mother, as she moved through her 80s. That's when we have to be doubly mindful, though, because by repressing our emotions and letting our frustrations fester, we're more likely to have an emotional outburst. It's truly a double-edged sword.

Some of the ways to deal with these feelings and create a positive dialogue with your older loved ones are to try and practice these communication techniques. Review this list of the five things _not_ to say:

1. *"How can you not remember that!?"* Even though you had two conversations about getting the car inspected and feel like the discussion was simple and memorable, to some folks, the conversation might as well have been last year. Seniors often lose short-term memory before long-term and forget all kinds of things we think are monumentally important, like where they put their glasses or keys — or when to take the car for maintenance and servicing to their mechanic.

   Say instead: *"See this sticker? Dad, if the car isn't inspected before the end of the month, we could have problems."* Place a few post-it notes around – on the dashboard, fridge and bathroom mirror. Add a smiley face to keep the tone light. And if you still think your parent might forget, make the appointment yourself and then call your dad that morning with a reminder.

2. *"You could do that if you really tried."* How hard is it to change the light bulb in the table lamp? Well, if your hands shake a lot or you can't reach the shelf where you keep spare bulbs, this task can become monumental. For some seniors, simple tasks, like tying shoes or changing lightbulbs, can become next to impossible if you have arthritis in your fingers or your back doesn't bend easily. Being shamed into doing something doesn't help anyone.

   Say instead: *"Let me watch and see where you're having trouble, so we can figure out how this can get done together."* Or if you live out of town, you could advise them to ask a friend, neighbor or other reliable person for help. Seniors, like everyone else, want to maintain their independence. But if a project is beyond their capabilities and they either don't know anyone who could help (or won't ask), you might need to step in to find someone who can lend a hand.

3. *"I just showed you how to use the remote control yesterday."* Learning new technology is tough (yes, even a new TV remote!) for

any adult, but gadgets with lots of buttons and options pose a special challenge for someone whose cognition or eyesight is failing. Even those of us with nimble fingers and well-functioning frontal lobes can be stymied by a new device that labels the controls differently from the one we are previously used to.

Say instead: *"The blue button on top turns the TV on, and there's one set of arrows for changing the channel and another for the volume. I'll show you."* Better yet, ask your parents' cable or satellite provider to recommend a senior-friendly remote control with a simple design. Some companies give these to seniors for a nominal charge. If not, purchase one at a local electronics store. Or if they're okay following instructions, you could write or print out step-by-step directions in large, legible type and leave it near the remote or listings guide.

4. *"What does that have to do with what we're talking about?"* One minute you and your dad are discussing baseball and the next he's talking about a problem with the dishwasher. What happened? Conversations with elderly parents often "go rogue," either because they can't keep their mind on the thread or they are simply bored and want to change the subject.

    Say instead: *"I was telling you about the game last night. Let's talk about the dishwasher in a minute."* If the subject is important to you, try to bring the conversation back on track without pointing a finger at your parent. To avoid suppressing genuine anger or sadness, gently explain why the conversation was important to you. Another option: Say nothing and just listen.

5. **"You already told me that."** And you don't ever repeat yourself? We all say things more than once but because elderly parents seem to do it all the time, we lose our patience with them. Be patient. We know our time is limited and we have many other responsibilities but some day we may miss the repetition of that same old story.

    Say instead: *"No kidding?! And don't tell me that the next thing you did was …"* Yes, you can make a joke out of it but only if your parent won't feel hurt. Best-case scenario: Your mom or dad will feel amused and relaxed enough to join in.

I hope these dialogue tips are helpful. Make your dialogue with your folks loving and as much fun as possible. You never know how many of these talks you may have left.

Now What?

Congratulations! After all your hard work, your loved one accepts the idea that a little extra help is a good idea. The question now becomes, "How do I find a reliable, quality personal care home health company to care for my loved one?" I would like to close this chapter with some useful information and a few ideas to help you find the best personal home care company for all people involved. This is a key step in helping your loved one stay safe and secure.

First, let me share an article by Jane Wilkens Michael, a wonderful writer and the author of *Long Live You!* Jane interviewed me for the following article that appeared in *Spry Magazine*. I believe you will find it helpful.

Protect Your Family When Hiring an In-Home Healthcare Worker
By Jane Wilkens Michael

It's a topic most people don't want to think about, especially when they're young, vibrant and feeling invincible. Eventually, though, it's something we must all give thought to: our needs and the needs of our loved ones as we get older — or worse, suffer a debilitating condition.

More specifically, what will happen to a loved one when taking care of him becomes too much for the primary caregiver? Will he be moved to a nursing home or other long-term-care facility, or might he be able to stay in the comfort of his own home?

In-home healthcare workers play an important role in keeping a loved one at home, but the industry has faced some bad publicity in the last year alone. One of the most shocking cases happened just two months ago in Detroit. A home healthcare worker was supposed to be caring *for an 80-year-old woman with dementia. Instead, she was only taking care of herself, allegedly stealing more than $1.5 million from the family that hired her. Not only was the caregiver severely neglecting her client; there was even a warrant for her arrest before she even got the job.*

How can this happen?

"It shouldn't," says Kurt Kazanowski, the founder of Homewatch CareGivers *and a healthcare executive with more than three decades of experience. "This horrifying story demonstrates how vulnerable the elderly can be and how naive some families are when hiring a caregiver or home care agency."*

Kazanowski says in general, the home healthcare industry is full of dedicated professionals who truly love what they do and are making a difference for those for whom they provide care. "It's a classic case of a few bad apples giving the entire industry a bad reputation," he says. "Consumers can take some simple measures when hiring an in-home healthcare worker."

Background Checks

In the Detroit case, Kazanowski says the agency failed to complete a background check on its employee. And he says one background check before the worker is hired isn't enough. Employers should complete background checks every six months, and these checks should include a motor vehicle background review – something that some background checks don't include. "Unfortunately, good people turn bad, and bad people can only hide for so long. That's why on-going background checks are essential," he says. "In addition to background checks, always speak to other families that your healthcare worker provided care for and get their feedback."

Shop Around

Hiring an in-home healthcare worker is one of the most important decisions a family can make. Even if the healthcare worker comes highly recommended and has an impressive resume, the match needs to feel like a good one to the family and especially the patient. "I always tell people it's like buying a car, only more important," Kazanowski says. "You wouldn't buy the first car you test drive, so why in the world would you settle on the first home healthcare company you find or meet with?"

Meet Ahead of Time

Once you find an in-home healthcare agency with which you are comfortable, the next step is meeting with the person who will actually be providing the care. "Insist on meeting the actual healthcare worker who you will be letting into your home," Kazanowski says. "The problem is most families just meet with an administrator or salesman from the company, not the actual healthcare provider. This isn't good enough. Any reputable in-home healthcare agency will accommodate this request. And make sure to meet prior to the first day on the job in case any issues or concerns need to be addressed."

Quality Assurance Checks

You probably remember gritting your teeth and the heart palpations when you faced a pop quiz back in high school. For a home healthcare worker, quality assurance checks are no different. Kazanowski says some are scheduled, some are unscheduled and all are in place to make sure the in-home healthcare workers are following the care plan.

"A reputable in-home healthcare agency will provide regular quality assurance checks or 'spot visits' to check on the caregiver and make sure all is well in the home," he says. "It ensures that your loved one is properly cared for, bathed frequently, takes medication as prescribed and is living in a clean and healthy environment."

Status Reports and Point of Contact

Most caregivers and the families they serve develop a strong bond: The worker becomes like family to the loved ones of the person they care for. Sometimes you can address very minor issues directly with the worker. Still, a reputable in-home healthcare agency should provide you an easy-to-reach company contact to discuss any concerns. In addition, regular status reports should be provided by the healthcare company to the spouse or immediate family of the person receiving care.

"These status reports are like an update or a progress report on how the patient is doing, what can be improved on and addresses other concerns the healthcare worker has," Kazanowski says. "The reality is that most relationships are a great match, and very rarely do any surprises arise as part of these status updates. But they are a good way to document that the care plan is being followed."

Family Involvement
The most important piece of advice that Kazanowski gives his own clients: Family members must be involved and keep tabs on what's going on.

"Keep an eye on credit card statements, checking and savings account balances and other important financial documents," he says. "Have mail forwarded to the children of the elderly family member. Children should make unannounced visits to the home. And ask the home care worker to provide receipts if he or she does grocery shopping or makes any purchases on behalf of your loved one."

The need for in-home care will continue to be in demand, especially as the aging of America crests in 2030. With some due diligence, it is very possible to find an in-home healthcare company that will provide excellent care and give you peace of mind while providing your loved one with safety, security and a sense of independence.

Helpful Resources
Jane's article above provides some good advice as you start a search for the right personal home care company for you. Some families I meet with tell me, "We can hire a caregiver for half the price you are offering." I tell the family, "Yes, you can! But be careful. You usually get what you pay for." Then I give them several stories from newspapers of families who have hired caregivers without doing things Jane suggested in her article and have had

very bad experiences. An article on the front page of the *Detroit News* and *Free Press* about a caregiver case, "A Cautionary Tale," on Sunday, Aug. 24, 2014, illustrates my point. Another great online resource to find a high-quality caregiving company is Caring.com. This web-based resource can help you get started.

Finally, the following is a list of 10 questions to consider and ask as you interview caregivers and caregiver companies.

10 Questions to Ask Before Hiring a Home Care Provider

When selecting a home care agency, it's important to know what questions to ask. Here are some examples of important questions that consumers should ask of a prospective service provider:

1. How long has the agency been providing private home care?
2. Is a written, customized care plan developed in consultation with the client and family members, and is the plan updated as changes occur?
3. How are emergencies handled after normal business hours?
4. Does the agency closely supervise the quality of care, including maintenance of a daily journal in the client's home and non-scheduled supervisory visits?
5. Does the agency employ a nurse, social worker or other qualified professionals to make regular visits to the client's home?
6. Does the agency provide a written document that states the rights of the patient and the responsibilities of the client, and explains the company's privacy policy and code of ethics?
7. Does the agency triple-screen their caregiver employees carefully, including use of reference checks, driving records and criminal background investigations?
8. Does the agency mandate ongoing training of its employees to continually update their skills?
9. Does the agency manage all payroll and employee-related matters and adhere to state and federal guidelines in its employment

practices, such as withholding appropriate taxes and providing Workers' Compensation and other benefits?

10. Does the agency also use independent contractors? If so, who employs the person and what type of background checks do they do on these contractors? Also, who pays the mandated taxes and withholding?

These important questions will provide a better and more critical view of what to expect from a personal home care company. A thorough review of the answers will give you an idea of the caliber of care that they will provide to your loved ones.

CHAPTER 3

Dealing With Your Parents' Dementia or Alzheimer's Disease

My mother started to have short-term memory issues at age 83, three years before she died. Unfortunately, this is all too common an occurrence as we age. One day, while I was at my brother's house visiting my mom, my brother Garrett told me Mom was starting to become forgetful, mostly in the form of asking the same questions over and over again. For example, she would ask, "Did the mail come?" and it had come. Or, "Did Karla call?" and Karla had called just an hour ago, and, "Is it time for dinner?" and she had just finished eating. Mom's long-term memory was still strong, thankfully. Mom didn't have Alzheimer's but nonetheless, her memory was starting to diminish.

Seeing all these changes occurring in Mom during her 80s was unsettling to me, and, I must admit, I was in a state of denial with most of them. The thought of my mother starting to decline in any way was upsetting to me. I felt helpless! Denial was my defense mechanism. Unfortunately, "Denial isn't just a river in Egypt." Denial, for me, however, was a much cleaner and easier way for me to deal with what was happening to my mother. My brother, on the other hand, was much more realistic and in tune than I was to what was going on with our mom. I guess living with her made it hard to avoid the signs and symptoms. My brother Garrett actually helped me be more comfortable with the changes occurring in Mom.

There again, my training as a nurse and working in healthcare all my life did not prepare me for how to deal with my mother's memory loss and all the resentment and bad feelings I had as my mother was slowly slipping away. This reminded me again how people with no medical or healthcare experience must feel. I was really lost!

I've always felt that the first step in gaining a handle on any new challenge is to arm yourself with knowledge and not let ignorance, fear and denial lead you down a path of wrong decisions.

This chapter is intended to help you deal with a loved one with memory loss issues. This process all starts with you getting in touch with your own feelings, as this is the critical first step in helping you manage the challenges ahead. I also will provide you with some useful facts and information, as well as helpful tips and resources to help you through this difficult time. The main thing is, you are not alone anymore!

Dementia vs. Alzheimer's Disease

Several of the first few patients we helped when I opened *Homewatch* in 2005 had Dementia. I remember receiving a call one day from Mrs. Adler, who was the only daughter of her parents, Bessy and Ben, ages 85 and 88, respectively. Mrs. Adler was calling for help, as her parents, who lived by themselves, were having memory loss issues. In addition, Bessy was just diagnosed with Dementia. Mrs. Adler's concerns were twofold: First, the safety and well-being of her parents, and second, her own well-being, as she was starting to experience caregiver burnout from the daily rigor of helping her parents. She was calling to arrange for a caregiver to come into the house three days per week for four hours at a time to assist her with this difficult situation.

As usual with our process at *Homewatch*, I set up a time to make a home visit to complete an assessment and start the process to find a caregiver just right for Mrs. Adler's parents. We agreed to meet the following day over at her parents' house. I met her there as planned. As I was talking with her, she asked me a question I couldn't clearly answer. "Kurt, my mother's doctor says my mother has Dementia. Does that mean she has Alzheimer's disease?"

Gee, where was all my nursing training when I needed it? I replied to Mrs. Adler, "I am embarrassed to say I am not 100 percent sure. I will go back to my office when I am finished here and make sure I get you the correct answer." While that satisfied Mrs. Adler for the moment, I still felt ill-prepared not knowing the answer.

I went back to my office and immediately called a good friend of mine who is a Geriatric physician, a doctor specializing in the diseases and conditions of seniors. Beth, a good friend and an excellent physician, gave me a brief "101 course" in memory loss. She provided me with an overview of the differences between Dementia and Alzheimer's disease. I called Mrs. Adler that evening and actually spent an hour on the phone with her and her husband going over the information they requested. During our time on the phone, I helped educate them about the differences between the two, reducing their fears and giving them more confidence on how to care and support Bessy and Ben best.

I started by saying that many people use the words "Dementia" and "Alzheimer's disease" interchangeably. However, they're *not* the same thing. You can have a form of Dementia that is completely unrelated to Alzheimer's disease. Mrs. Adler then stated, "So, all Alzheimer's is Dementia, but not all Dementia is Alzheimer's, right?"

"Correct," I replied. I went on to say that Dementia isn't a disease. It's a group of symptoms that affect mental tasks like memory and reasoning. Dementia can be caused by a variety of conditions, the most common of which is Alzheimer's disease.

I told Mrs. Adler that as Dementia progresses, it can have a devastating impact on the ability to function independently, such as she was experiencing with her mother. It's a major cause of disability for older people, and places an emotional and financial burden on families and caregivers.

Mrs. Adler went on to tell me the early symptoms of Dementia for her mother started with simple episodes of forgetfulness. I told her that people with Dementia have trouble keeping track of time and tend to lose their way in familiar settings. As Dementia progresses, forgetfulness and confusion grow. It becomes harder for the person with Dementia to recall names and faces. Personal care becomes a problem.

Obvious signs of Dementia include repetitious questioning, inadequate hygiene and poor decision-making. In the most advanced stage, Dementia patients become unable to care for themselves. Time, places and recognizing people become much more difficult and confusing. Behavior continues to change and can turn into depression and aggression.

As I spoke with Mrs. Adler and her husband, I could tell that they felt Bessy had started to experience Dementia much earlier than they thought.

Our dialogue shifted to Alzheimer's disease. I proceeded to explain that Alzheimer's is a progressive disease of the brain that slowly impairs memory and cognitive functions. The exact cause is unknown and there is no cure, poor treatments and few options to try to prevent the disease. I cited some information from the National Institutes of Health (NIH) estimating that more than five million people in the United States have Alzheimer's disease. Although younger people can (and do) get Alzheimer's, symptoms generally begin after age 60. We ended our talk discussing how Alzheimer's disease is usually fatal. The time from diagnosis to death can be as little as three years in people over 80 years old. However, it can be much longer for younger people. According to the Alzheimer's Association, Alzheimer's disease is the sixth leading cause of death in the United States, implicated in about 83,000 deaths annually.

The Adlers now had a better understanding of what was going on with Mrs. Adler's parents and this helped in clarifying the expected progression of Bessie's Dementia. The old adage of "knowledge is power" seemed to hold true here. One of the best tools to help you deal with the challenges your loved ones are facing is knowledge. Having the resources you need will strengthen your understanding and empowerment.

Back to my home assessment of the Adlers: Bessy and Ben were a lovely elderly couple. Married 61 years, you could still feel the love between them. Bessy's Dementia was a little more advanced than I originally thought and I could tell Ben was both frightened and sad about how to help his wife best and what the immediate future may hold. I could also feel the same concerns from their daughter. I completed my assessment and then created a Care Plan for Bessie. I was able to line up a caregiver named Emily, who lived right around the corner from Bessy and Ben. Emily was a mature, sensitive woman with a very patient personality; perfect for helping care for a person with Dementia. Mrs. Adler was pleased, and for the moment, all was good.

The Hard Facts about Dementia

To help wrap your thinking and feelings around Dementia, you should know that Dementia is a syndrome, usually of a chronic or progressive nature, caused by a variety of brain illnesses that affect memory, thinking, behavior and the ability to perform everyday activities.

The number of people living with Dementia worldwide is currently estimated at 35.6 million. This number is expected to double by 2030 and more than triple by 2050. In Moscow, Russia, and Guangzhou, China, where I visit often, the challenges in dealing with Dementia are the same as in the United States. Dementia is a global issue.

Dementia is overwhelming not only for the people who have it, but also for their caregivers, co-workers and families. The lack of awareness and understanding of Dementia in most countries results in stigmatization and barriers to diagnosis and care, impacting caregivers, families and societies physically, psychologically and economically.

The World Health Organization (WHO) offers these 10 sobering facts on Dementia:

1. Dementia is not a normal part of aging. Although Dementia mainly affects older people, it is not a normal part of getting older.
2. More than 35 million people suffer from Dementia worldwide (2010 figures). Among them, 58 percent live in low and middle income countries, and this proportion is projected to rise to 71 percent by 2050.
3. A new case of Dementia is diagnosed every 4 seconds. The total number of new cases of Dementia each year worldwide is nearly 7.7 million. The number of people with Dementia is expected to nearly double every 20 years to 65.7 million in 2030 and 115.4 million in 2050.
4. Dementia has a huge economic impact; in the United States alone, the costs associated with treating people diagnosed with Dementia amount to approximately $604 billion per year. The high cost of

the disease will challenge health systems to deal with the predicted future increase of cases. The costs are expected to increase even more quickly, due to the prevalence of the disease.

5. Caregivers of Dementia patients experience high strain. Caring for Dementia patients is overwhelming for caregivers, who report physical, emotional and economic stress. Caregivers require support from the health, social, financial and legal systems.

6. Early diagnosis improves the quality of life of people with Dementia and their families. The principal goals for Dementia care are:

   - Diagnosing cases early;
   - Optimizing physical health, cognition, activity and well-being;
   - Detecting and treating behavioral and psychological symptoms; and
   - Providing information and long-term support to caregivers.

7. People with Dementia and their families are often discriminated against. People with Dementia are frequently denied the basic rights and freedoms available to others. For example, physical and chemical restraints are used extensively in aged-care facilities and acute-care settings.

8. More research and evaluation is required to develop new and more effective treatments and to understand the causes of Dementia better. Research that identifies the modifiable risk factors of Dementia is still scarce.

9. Dementia is a public health priority. To address this, the following actions can be taken:

   - We can promote a Dementia-friendly society;
   - We can make Dementia a public health and social care priority everywhere;
   - We can improve attitudes toward, and further our understanding of, Dementia;
   - We can invest in health and social systems to improve care and services for people with Dementia and their caregivers; and
   - We can increase the number of research studies on Dementia.

10. Dementia caregivers need our support: More than 10 million Americans face the task of caring for a family member with Dementia. About one in four caregivers devote 40 hours a week providing care for a parent or loved one with Dementia. In dealing with a parent suffering with Dementia, you need support from family members, friends, experts and paid caregivers.

Understanding these 10 points will empower you to support your loved one with Dementia and help you deal with your own feelings. The resources at the end of this chapter will help translate your understanding into positive actions.

True Love and Understanding

As many caregivers will tell you, it's not easy to deal with a parent with Dementia or its most common type, Alzheimer's disease. About 75 percent of the clients we care for at *Homewatch* have some form of Dementia. At my company, we receive calls every day from family members attempting to care for a loved one with some form of Dementia.

The following are some interviews I've completed with family members who have firsthand knowledge of what it's like caring for a loved one experiencing some form of memory loss. We at *Homewatch Caregivers* have had the honor and privilege of caring for their loved ones. I hope their words and expressions of love will be an inspiration to you.

"No one understands it until they've been through it. Some Dementia patients either don't realize that they have a problem or refuse to believe or acknowledge it. This is very common. There is no point in trying to convince your parent of the Dementia, as it will only lead to defensiveness and unhappiness for both of you. Please realize that there's still that voice inside your parent that tells him that he wants to be independent and do things his own way. He doesn't want to be ordered around by his children. Dealing with your parent will require patience and restraint on your part. By patience, I mean being willing to wait until your parent actually asks for your help. And by restraint, I mean holding your tongue when you're tempted to argue. You will

never win this argument. With my own mother, I found that if I could make her think that the good ideas were actually her ideas, she was much more willing to cooperate with things like taking her medications and bathing. Is there a possibility that you could hire someone to come in and stay with your parent for a couple of mornings or afternoons per week? If so, that would give you some time to yourself, which I'm sure you really need." – Ms. Pepper, Utica, Michigan

"My mother had Dementia, and she lived with my husband and me. It was so difficult to deal with. She didn't deny that she had Dementia, she just didn't know it. She would forget that she was forgetful. For example, I would make her dinner. She would eat and then go to her bedroom only to come back out a few minutes later and ask me if I was ever going to feed her. No one can understand what it is like unless you have been the caregiver for someone with Dementia. My brother and sister knew, but it didn't affect them as they only saw her for an hour or two maybe once a week. Bless anyone who takes care of their parents, and just remember to take care of you, too. I was so happy my neighbor made the suggestion of trying to find someone to come in and help once in a while! A God-sent excellent suggestion. I got to the point that my eyes twitched, and my heart skipped beats because of the stress." – Mrs. Nagy, Farmington Hills, Michigan

"I take care of people with Dementia on a daily basis in the hospital in which I work and also took care of my grandmother, who had it before she died. The only advice I can give to others when trying to work with someone who has Dementia is to live in their world. I know that sounds hard for most of us but it really makes the simplest things manageable. If they want to talk about things that make no sense to you, don't correct them, for this will make it hard on them and on you. Just go with their conversation. Also, I have noticed that when it's time to bathe a person with this disease, do not place a dark colored bath mat in the tub. To someone with Dementia, it appears to them as being a dark hole in the tub. Let the person you are caring for undress themselves with some assistance from you. Make it out as a game of sorts. This will work best to control anger and confusion. Another bit of advice to you is to love them. Denial is what they know, so, of

course, they won't admit to having anything wrong, mentally. Just breathe. Enjoy all the time you have left with the ones you love. Again, live in their world, don't make them live in yours." – Mrs. Pas, Westland, Michigan

The Task of Being a Family Caregiver

Starting with what I learned from my mother as she lost her memory and then from all the families at *Homewatch* we have cared for, being a family caregiver for a loved one with Dementia is truly a labor of love. The following passage is something I bet will sound very familiar if you have a loved one with Dementia.

When a parent has Dementia, your whole world changes! The family caregiver often has to help out with ordinary household tasks, provide personal care, and perform other services and functions. It can be the equivalent of a full-time job. Indeed, the Alzheimer's Association says about 25 percent of family caregivers devote about 40 hours a week in service to the parent or loved one.

The family caregiver may often be forced to intervene in the personal life of the parent – a very unpleasant but necessary thing to do. As symptoms of impairment from Dementia worsen, the caregiver may have to make decisions on behalf of the parent. For instance, as we talked about in Chapter Two, driving a car may no longer be safe, and the family caregiver may have to take away the car keys despite possible objections from the parent.

One time, when I made a home visit to sign up an elderly man for *Homewatch* services, his daughter told me, "When a parent has Dementia, the family caregiver often has to help out with daily household tasks, provide personal care, and perform other services. People don't truly understand that fact! It can be the equivalent of a full-time job. My brother and sister-in-law all of a sudden had another full-time job."

Caring for a parent with Dementia can be a daunting challenge. Very often, a family member decides to provide the care personally. As the parent's condition worsens, he or she will require progressively more assistance. The toll on the family caregiver's physical, social and mental health can be steep, and there may be adverse consequences on work, relationships, finances and his/her own family life. Being a caregiver for a loved one with Dementia or

Alzheimer's disease causes caregiver burnout faster and more intensely than caring for loved ones with other conditions.

The American Geriatrics Society says that caregivers should include provisions for getting relief in their program of care. Unless the family caregiver gets enough relief and support, he or she runs a higher risk of illness, anxiety and depression. We discussed caregiver burnout in Chapter One, and it's not something to be taken lightly!

Helpful Tips in Dealing with a Parent with Dementia

There are three basic things to consider in dealing with a parent with Dementia:

1. **Learn as much as possible about the condition.** Nothing experienced in adult life prepares a person to care for a parent or loved one with Dementia. I couldn't agree more from my experience with my own mother. The person looks exactly the same, making it difficult to imagine that the brain is progressively deteriorating and mental faculties are changing. However, because the condition lasts for years, there is enough time for the family to research the disease and develop knowledge of what to expect. With more knowledge, the family caregiver can improve the quality of care for the parent and reduce the personal stress associated with caring for a parent with Dementia.

2. **Get as much help as possible.** There is one thing the family caregiver must realize: It's not possible to do it alone. Recognizing caregiver burnout on your part and dealing with it directly is imperative. You'll need help from as many resources as possible: family members and other relatives, friends, doctors and other experts, and paid caregivers. *Homewatch Caregivers* and other similar personal home care companies are just such a resource. The stress from dealing with a parent with Dementia is considerably more than one can imagine, and studies show it can affect personal health, well-being and relationships.

3. **Make sure paid caregivers have Dementia training.** Whether hiring caregivers to provide personal care for a parent at home or moving the parent to a full-time care facility, be certain that the caregivers are suitably trained. A loved one with Dementia can be expected to

exhibit difficult behavior. The paid caregiver needs to have a depth of understanding that comes with good training to be able to provide the proper care necessary to deal with difficult patients in a respectful manner. The techniques for successfully working with Dementia patients do not come naturally; they need to be learned.

Dealing with Dementia Behavior Problems

Over the past year, *Homewatch* has worked with many families whose loved ones are experiencing Dementia and Alzheimer's disease. In our work, we have identified a few common themes related to care challenges that I wanted to share with you here. Most importantly, by showing some common situations, you can pick up some helpful Dementia care dos and don'ts.

Mid-to-late stage Dementia and Alzheimer's patients often present challenging behavior problems for their caregivers. Families have a difficult time facing these behaviors when their loved ones experience extreme mood swings, including anger, sadness, paranoia, confusion and fear. These emotions can result in oppositional, aggressive and sometimes violent speech or actions. Understanding and learning which strategies are most effective greatly assists with Dementia behavior management.

Communication difficulties can be one of the most upsetting aspects of caring for someone with Alzheimer's disease or some other type of Dementia – and it can be frustrating for the patient as well as for family members. Seeing a loved one who once was a strong and expressive person in an altered state is quite distressing. Although it can be hard to understand why people with Dementia act the way they do, the explanation is attributable to their disease and the changes it causes in the brain. Familiarize yourself with some of these common situations that arise when someone has Dementia, so that if your loved one says something shocking or puzzling, you'll know how to respond calmly and effectively.

Common Situations with Dementia

Common Situation #1: Aggressive Speech or Actions – Statements, such as, "I don't want to take a shower!" "I want to go home!" or "I don't want to eat that!" may escalate into aggressive behavior.

Explanation: The most important thing to remember about verbal or physical aggression, says the Alzheimer's Association, is that your loved one is not doing it on purpose. Aggression is usually triggered by something, often physical discomfort, environmental factors, such as being in an unfamiliar situation, or even poor communication. A lot of times, aggression is coming from pure fear.

DO: Try to identify the cause of the behavior. The key to responding to aggression caused by Dementia is to identify what the person is feeling to make him or her behave aggressively. Once you've made sure the loved one isn't in danger (or putting anyone else in danger), you can try to shift the focus to something else, speaking in a calm, reassuring manner.

DON'T: Try to forcibly restrain the person unless there is absolutely no choice. The worst thing you can do is engage in an argument or force the issue that's creating the aggression. This is so important! Most professionals agree the best way to stop aggressive behavior is to remove the word "no" from your vocabulary.

Common Situation #2: Confusion about Time or Place – Statements such as, "This isn't my house," "When are we leaving?" or "Why are we here?" are very common with Dementia and Alzheimer's patients.

Explanation: Wanting to go home is one of the most common reactions for an Alzheimer's or Dementia patient living in a care facility. Alzheimer's causes progressive damage to cognitive functioning, and this is what creates the confusion and memory loss.

DO: Respond with simple explanations when your loved one's questions indicate confusion. There are a few possible ways to respond when your loved one is confused about where he or she is. The Alzheimer's Association suggests simple explanations, along with photos and other tangible reminders, can help. Sometimes, however, it can be better to redirect the person, particularly when you're in the process of moving your loved one to a facility or other location. The better solution here, according to the experts, may be to say as little as possible about the fact that they have all of their belongings packed and instead try to redirect them – find another activity, go for a walk, get a snack, etc. If your loved one asks specific questions, such as, "When are we leaving?" you might respond with, "We can't leave until later because the traffic is terrible/the forecast is calling for bad weather/or it's too late to leave tonight."

DON'T: Try to reason with someone who has Alzheimer's or Dementia. Lengthy explanations or reasons are not the way to go. It just can't be done.

Common Situation #3: Poor Judgment or Cognitive Problems – You may hear unfounded allegations from your loved one with Alzheimer's disease or Dementia, such as "She stole my vacuum cleaner!" You also may notice trouble with math or finances, such as not being able to figure out the tip on a restaurant bill. Other examples include unexplained hoarding or stockpiling and repetition of statements or tasks.

Explanation: The deterioration of brain cells caused by Alzheimer's is a particular culprit in behaviors showing poor judgment or errors in thinking. These can contribute to delusions or untrue beliefs. Some of these problems are obvious, such as when someone is hoarding household items, or accuses a family member of stealing something. Some are more subtle, however, and the person may not realize that they are having trouble with things that they never used to think twice about.

Being Aware of the Warning Signs

As we discussed, Alzheimer's disease is the most common form of Dementia in the elderly. But there are several other factors, too. Dementia strikes individuals with poorly controlled diabetes, high blood pressure, high cholesterol and heart disease. Even worse, as patients begin to decline, they can be at risk for vascular Dementia, which is caused by a series of small strokes that damage or destroy brain tissue and prevent oxygen from reaching the brain. Vascular Dementia is a serious health concern for older adults. High blood pressure is an especially important risk factor but thankfully it's one that can be controlled! It's vital to monitor your loved one's blood pressure level regularly. If it's high, consult with and follow their doctor's recommendations for treatment.

Because strokes occur suddenly, symptoms of vascular Dementia may develop unexpectedly or without warning, or remain constant for a period of time and then abruptly become worse. Individuals with vascular Dementia may even appear to improve for short intervals, only to get worse after the occurrence of one or more additional strokes. It is also possible for a person to suffer from both vascular Dementia and Alzheimer's disease simultaneously.

Many people may be too embarrassed to discuss it or simply unaware that they've developed Dementia. Most people are aware something is going on with them. So it is important to know the warning signs. If you observe a sudden development of any of the following symptoms, it may signal the onset of vascular Dementia:

- Confusion and short-term memory loss;
- Wandering or lost in familiar places;
- Shuffling gait;
- Loss of bladder or bowel control;
- Failure to thrive;
- Laughing or crying inappropriately;
- Difficulty following instructions; or
- Problems managing money.

When Caregiver Intervention Is Needed

Keep a close eye on your loved ones and don't let Dementia rob them of their enjoyment for life. If you notice any of the warning signs above, contact your loved one's physician, a quality Geriatric Assessment Center or hospital for evaluation.

At *Homewatch*, we were caring for a woman who started to show several of these signs and symptoms. Our caregiver called our company nurse and we worked with the family to get their mother an appointment at a Geriatric Assessment Center at a local hospital. If you suspect your loved one may be experiencing vascular Dementia:

1. Schedule a doctor's visit. Ask the physician what physical and mental function tests can be done to diagnose the possible Dementia as well as the underlying causes.
2. Follow the doctor's recommendations and schedule your family member for the appropriate diagnostic tests. When a diagnosis has been made, consult with the doctor to determine the best course of treatment.
3. Check your loved one's blood sugar level daily and, if needed, manage diabetes carefully. Poorly controlled diabetes is a serious risk

factor for vascular Dementia (and other dire consequences), so it is critical that your loved one receives proper diabetes care.

I have one closing piece of advice: Go with your gut. This feeling is usually correct.

The Art of Communicating

During my work in healthcare over the past three decades, I have heard many people use the phrase, "empty shell of a person," when describing a loved one devastated by the later stages of Dementia. Sadly, Dementia does indeed transform people into shadows of their former selves, but those living with Dementia are far from "empty shells." Yes, the shell may become more and more difficult to open. Some days it might not open at all. But never forget that there is a beautiful, unvarnished pearl within your loved one.

Understanding how to "open the shell" gives you the opportunity to meaningfully connect with your loved one affected by Dementia. Just as the right tools and a lot of technique is required to open an oyster, there are techniques and creative ways to communicate or connect emotionally with your loved one who has Dementia.

For your consideration and use, here are 10 tips on how to communicate effectively with your loved one who has moderate to severe Dementia:

1. **Recognize what you're up against**. Dementia inevitably gets worse with time. People with Dementia will gradually have a more difficult time understanding others, as well as communicating in general.
2. **Avoid distractions.** Try to find a place and time to talk when there aren't a lot of distractions present. This allows your loved one to focus all their mental energy on the conversation.
3. **Speak clearly and naturally in a warm and calm voice.** Refrain from "baby talk" or any other kind of condescension communication.
4. **Refer to your loved one by his or her name**. Avoid pronouns like "he," "she" and "they" during conversation. Names are also important when greeting a loved one with Dementia. For example: "Hello, Mom. It's me, Kurt," is preferred over, "Hello, it's me."

5. **Talk about one thing at a time.** Someone with Dementia may not be able to engage in the mental juggling involved in maintaining a conversation with multiple threads.

6. **Use nonverbal cues**. Maintain eye contact and smile. This helps put your loved one at ease and will facilitate understanding. And when Dementia is very advanced, nonverbal communication may be the only option available.

7. **Listen actively.** If you don't understand something your loved one is telling you, politely let him or her know and ask for more details.

8. **Don't argue.** Your conversations are not likely to go very far if you try to correct every inaccurate statement your loved one makes. It's okay to let delusions and misstatements go.

9. **Have patience.** Give your loved one extra time to process what you say. If you ask a question, give him or her a moment to respond. Don't let frustration get the better of you. Remember this is not about you.

10. **Understand there will be good days and bad days.** While the general trend of Dementia sufferers is a downward decline, people with Dementia will have ups and downs just like anyone else.

Helpful Resources on Dementia and Alzheimer's Disease

The following are some helpful websites I've found to help you learn more about Dementia and Alzheimer's disease:

- The National Institutes of Health (NIH) National Institute on Aging site explains both Alzheimer's disease and vascular Dementia and offers resources for caregivers: **www.nia.nih.gov/Alzheimers/default.htm**
- Download a vascular Dementia fact sheet from the NIH: **www.nia.nih.gov/Alzheimers/Publications/Dementia.htm**
- The Alzheimer's Society in Great Britain has an excellent site for caregivers: **www.alzheimers.org.uk**
- The Merck manual of Geriatrics offers a collection of articles on Dementia and Alzheimer's disease: **www.merck.com**

Other Resources

When the time comes to look for assistance in the form of a caregiver to help out, these are some excellent resources to have at your disposal.

- CareInHomes: **www.careinhomes.com**
- A Place for Mom: **www.aplaceformom.com**
- Caring.Com: **www.caring.com**
- *Homewatch CareGivers*: **www.homewatchcaregivers.com**
- CareFinderPros: **www.carefinderpros.com; Dr.Mike@carefinder-pros.com**

Whether you are just beginning your journey or are an experienced caregiver, I hope this chapter brought you some useful insights and helpful tools to make your life and the life of your loved one richer.

CHAPTER 4

The Beginning of the End – "The Fall"

I will remember this day forever. It was Monday, June 11, 2012, and a beautiful summer morning. I was in my office enjoying my second cup of green tea when my mobile phone rang. It was 11:10 a.m. and the display showed it was my brother's home phone number. A flash of panic went through me, as I knew my brother was working, and Mom was home alone that day at the house where she lived with my brother. I quickly answered the phone and my mother said, "Son, I fell and hurt myself. Please come here now." Her voice was shaky and I could hear the fear in her voice. I remember I became faint and nearly passed out from a surge of panic in my body. I have never heard my mother's voice like that and it scared the hell out of me!

I called my brother at work and then drove right over to their place with a staff person from my office. My mother was sitting on the sofa in her robe with a small gash in her forehead and her face all covered with blood. I nearly fainted again. I couldn't tell how bad she was hurt or whether she had broken any bones. My mom was shaking all over, as the fall had totally frightened her. I remember I nearly started to cry, not so much for what had just happened to her but for the fact I saw my mother as I have never seen her before. She was so vulnerable looking. I knew she was hurt and could only imagine her fear and what she was going through. As a nurse, I also knew that falls are usually the start of a sequence of decline in some seniors.

I asked my mother what happened and in a disoriented voice, she said that she opened the front door and walked outside to get the newspaper, which was on the front porch. "I just stumbled and fell," my mom told me. She appeared to have tripped and fell very hard right down on her face. She managed to get her arm under her to slightly support herself, but otherwise, it was a direct hit!

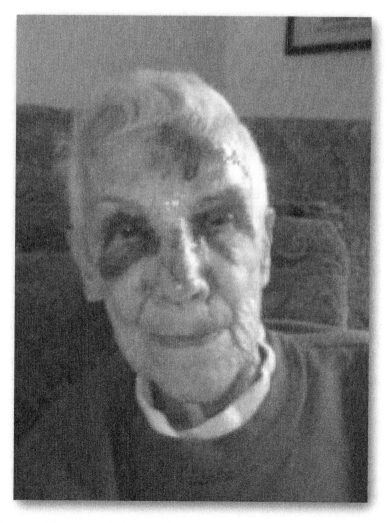

My mom's fall represented a big wakeup call to all of us. Thankfully – no broken bones!

"I was able to crawl back into the house," she went on to say. I truly don't know how she managed to do that, let alone how she got back on the sofa and called me at work.

As I was wiping away some of the blood and placing a bandage on her forehead and wrist, my brother got home and we took Mom to the hospital. She was severely bruised, her right wrist had a laceration on it, and it looked like she had been beaten. By the grace of God, however, she had no broken bones. Amazing! This event was an enormous wake-up call for my brother and me.

We knew it was not safe for Mom to be home alone any longer. We couldn't risk another fall ending with a broken hip or worse.

In my work as a personal care home health company owner, I had received many calls from families experiencing events like this one. Indeed, over the years, I've worked with hundreds of families who have called after their loved ones had fallen. Typically, when a senior falls and gets hurt, the family recognizes it's time to get a little extra help into the house. The fall results in a call to action. Families realize they can't dodge the bullet any further and start to take steps to prevent a life-threatening accident or severe injury from occurring. With some elderly folks who fall and break a bone, such as a hip, the injury turns out to be "the beginning of the end."

In fact, statistics reveal that falls in older people can be catastrophic. Falls are the **number-one** cause of injury and injury-related deaths in people over the age of 65!

In Canada, about 27,000 seniors suffer a hip fracture (broken hip) each year, incurring medical treatment costs of more than $1 billion; in the United States, there are 300,000 hip fractures by seniors annually. A quarter of the patients suffering hip fractures will die within a year, and half will suffer a major decline in independence, such as being forced to move from a home in the community to a long-term-care facility.

Some groundbreaking research completed in 2014 helps us understand better why elderly people fall. The findings were very surprising and we'll explore them together over the next few pages. Having a better understanding of why seniors fall can help families prevent them.

An Action Plan for Mom

The day following my mother's fall, my brother and I jumped into action and created a plan to help prevent Mom from falling and hurting herself again. The plan is the same that my company has used to help hundreds of other families.

Before you create a plan for your loved ones, you have to ask yourself a few important things. The first key question is: Will your loved one be home totally alone or will you have a professional caregiver and/or family member providing you with some support? This is important to answer factually, as it will directly affect to what degree you need to "fall proof" your loved one's home.

In the case of my brother and me, we decided to have a caregiver stay with my mother when Garrett was at work. Our caregiver Paula had worked with my company for several years and was a perfect match for my mother. Like most of the elderly folks we work with, my mother felt she didn't need a caregiver. But my brother and I told Mom (in a loving, caring way) that it wasn't an option. After a few weeks, Paula was like a member of the family and my mother learned to trust her. My brother worked three 12-hour shifts a week, which meant he was home four days a week. On the days Garrett worked, we had Paula come to the house and stay with my mother between the hours of 7 a.m. and 7 p.m. Garrett was with Mom at night and the rest of the time, except when I got a chance to come for a visit. So, in essence, my mother had someone with her all day, every day. Given how we structured my mom's care, here is what else we did to make the house safer:

1. We moved my mother's bed downstairs, so she didn't need to go up and down the stairs as much. Eliminating stairs from a senior's daily route helps decrease the risk of a fall. And when she did go up or down the stairs, it was ALWAYS with assistance.
2. We made the bathroom safer by adding grab bars in the bathtub and near the toilet and by removing the throw rugs, which are a common household hazard, contributing to slips and falls.
3. Mom exercised with her walker. Paula would make sure my mother walked around the house a few times a day to exercise her legs to maintain muscle tone.

4. We made sure Mom was hydrated. Dehydration in seniors can lead to being disoriented and contributing to falls.

5. We had mom's medications reviewed and adjusted by her physician.

If your loved one is determined to live alone, the second important question to answer is: Where can you locate some expertise to help you "fall proof" your loved one's home? At the end of this chapter and in Chapter Six, I'll give you some useful resources and helpful tips that can assist you with fall proofing, ranging from high-tech resources to basic common sense strategies or a combination of the two.

As people age, balance becomes a significant issue due to a variety of factors, including physical weakness, medications and cognitive or visual impairment. Ideally a source of comfort for aging loved ones, the home can become hazardous without a fall-prevention strategy. Later in this chapter, I will give you a few recommendations to take proactively to assess your loved one's home for anything that might be a health or fall risk. In addition, please consider helping your loved ones remain safe by:

- Checking on them regularly;
- Scheduling vision checks;
- Discussing medications with their physicians;
- Observing their balance and the way they get around; and
- Establishing light-exercise routines.

After observing any safety concerns, suggest an agreeable solution. We have several clients we care for that actually do yoga to help improve their strength and balance. Yoga is a wonderful low-impact exercise that also helps with relaxation, mood swings, breathing and more. It can be practiced at your own pace and level of fitness, so you don't have to be able to get into the Lotus position or Downward Dog to realize all the many benefits.

These are the key areas within the house to pay attention to when fall-proofing:

- Bedrooms
- Bathrooms
- Hallways

- Living Room
- Steps
- Kitchen
- External premises (yard, garden, driveway, etc.)

Why Do Older People Fall?

I came across the findings of a research project that I believe are worth sharing here. Stephen Robinovitch and his research team from Simon Fraser University completed a study in Canada in 2012. Contrary to popular assumption, poor reflexes or tripping may not be to blame for falls, according to this groundbreaking research. The study, published in *The Lancet* (one of the world's foremost medical journals), is the first to use digital video data from closed-circuit cameras installed in long-term-care facilities. The cameras were installed in various common areas, like living rooms and hallways, of two different nursing homes in British Columbia, Canada, with permission from the residents and staff. The aim of the research, according to Robinovitch, the principal author of the study, was to determine exactly what precipitated each fall, rather than relying on a questionnaire or so-called self-report after the fact, as previous studies have done.

A total of 227 falls among 130 residents were captured on video, and analyzed by Robinovitch's team at the university's Injury Prevention and Mobility Laboratory.

"This is the first study to collect objective evidence of the cause and circumstances of falls," Robinovitch says. "Previous data was collected anecdotally and depended on a person's memory of what caused them to fall or witnesses' memories, if there were any. We wanted to get video that would act like the black box in an airplane to determine what led to the crash."

The following are some of the key findings from the study (interesting stuff to say the least):

1. **What really causes falls:** While dizziness, medication side effects and certain health conditions like arrhythmias can contribute to falls, most falls in the past were attributed to simple "slips and trips," according to Robinovitch. The causes were determined by questioning the seniors themselves, or from laboratory reenactments of slipping, using much

younger subjects. But these external causes, like tripping over uneven surfaces or catching a foot on a chair leg or walker, only triggered about 20 percent of the falls in the Simon Fraser University study.

Much more common were falls caused by what the researchers call "incorrect transfer or shifting of bodyweight," which accounted for 41 percent of tumbles. These involved a body movement that caused the center of gravity to change improperly while walking or standing, and because it seemed intentional – or at least self-induced – the researchers describe the action as "internal" in origin. Many of these misjudgments or over-corrections occurred while transferring from a walker to a chair, or vice versa.

Only a very small proportion (3 percent) of falls were caused by slipping. While forward walking was one of the activities most commonly preceding a fall, so were sitting down and standing quietly. As I read these findings, it caused me to wonder what the true cause of my mother's fall was.

2. **Reaction time and bracing for a fall:** Though many people think an older person simply can't react quickly enough to break a fall or may not know they're falling until it's too late to prevent it, researchers discovered that was not typically the case.

    "A full 75 percent of the falls involved hand impact," Robinovitch says, "but it had no effect. In a way, this is good news: People have the reaction time, and the recognition that they're falling, so the arms reach out. The problem is that that action doesn't break their falls, which may be related to a lack of muscle strength in their upper body." I am sure this is what happened to my mother. She was able to react, as she managed to get her right arm and hand under her. She just didn't have the muscle strength to break the fall.

3. **Clues for prevention of falls:** Having precise information about which circumstances and actions lead to falls can help caregivers learn how to prevent them, according to Robinovitch. For example, the video can be used to show healthcare providers, like physiotherapists and occupational therapists, scenarios that cause problems for older adults with balance or mobility issues, helping to answer the question, "Why is my patient falling?" And since so many falls occurred as a person was leaving a walker to sit in a chair, or standing

from a chair to use a walker, Robinovitch suggests such assistive devices be modified to make those transitions easier.

Other research also has called for a redesign of conventional walkers, along with better education on how to use them safely. Here is another interesting tidbit of information: A 2009 review of admissions to emergency departments revealed that more than 47,000 older people are treated each year in the United States for falls associated with walkers and canes. Lead researcher and epidemiologist with the U.S. Centers for Disease Control and Prevention, Judy A. Stevens, writes that with 87 percent of those accidents involving walkers, women had a higher injury rate in all age categories. The study, published in the *Journal of the American Geriatrics Society*, also found that 60 percent of fall injuries happen at home, and only 16 percent in nursing homes.

Helping Keep the Johnsons' Home Safe and Secure

Mrs. Johnson called our *Homewatch* office inquiring about care for her husband Dan, who was 71 and had Parkinson's disease. Mrs. Johnson started our dialogue by saying her husband's disease had progressed to the point that he was not stable when walking. "My husband Dan is having more bad days than good. I'm concerned, especially when I am not there, that he may fall and hurt himself." I asked if Dan had a recent fall and Mrs. Johnson responded, "Dan fell while walking from the family room to the kitchen and hurt his arm. I think he has fallen a few other times but didn't tell me." I set up an evaluation visit the next day. During the visit, I was able to observe Mr. Johnson unstable on his feet. Mrs. Johnson was interested in having a caregiver at the house when she was not home, approximately three days per week for a three-to-four-hour period. While I was at the home, I did a fall assessment, as well. The next section will outline how I went about completing the fall assessment and the key questions you can ask yourself to assess your loved one's home.

Mr. Johnson agreed to have a caregiver come into the house when Mrs. Johnson was away from home. After a year of caregiving, Mr. Johnson has been kept safe, secure and independent in his house – fall free!

The following is the checklist I used at the Johnsons' home. The checklist reveals hazards that may be found in each room of your loved one's home. For each hazard, the checklist tells you how to fix the problem. At the end of the checklist, you'll find other tips for preventing falls.

FLOORS: Look at the floor in each room.

Q: When you walk through a room, do you have to walk around furniture? Move the furniture, so the path is clear.

Q: Do you have throw rugs on the floor? Remove the rugs or use double-sided tape or a non-slip backing, so the rugs won't slip.

Q: Are there papers, books, towels, shoes, magazines, boxes, blankets or other objects on the floor? Pick up these things and always keep objects off the floor and out of the walking path.

Q: Do you have to walk over or around wires or cords (like lamp, telephone or extension cords)? Coil or tape cords and wires next to the wall to avoid tripping over them. If needed, have an electrician put in another outlet.

STAIRS AND STEPS: Look at the stairs both inside and outside the home.

Q: Are there papers, shoes, books or other objects on the stairs? Pick up anything and always keep objects off stairs.

Q: Are some steps broken or uneven? Fix loose or uneven steps.

Q: Is the carpeting on the steps loose or torn? Make sure the carpet is firmly attached to every step, or remove the carpet and attach non-slip rubber treads to the stairs.

Q: Are you missing a light over the stairway? Have an electrician put in an overhead light at the top and bottom of the stairs.

Q: Do you have only one light switch for your stairs (only at the top or at the bottom of the stairs)? Have an electrician put in light switches at the top *and* bottom of the stairs. You also can get light switches that glow.

Q: Has the stairway light bulb burned out? Be sure to change the light bulbs as soon as possible. If necessary, ask a friend or family member for assistance.

Q: Are the handrails loose or broken? Is there a handrail on only one side of the stairs? Fix loose handrails or put in new ones. Make sure handrails are on both sides of the stairs and are as long as the stairs.

KITCHEN: Look at the kitchen and eating area.

Q: Are the cups, dishes and things used most often on high shelves? Move items used more frequently to the lower shelves of cabinets (about waist or shoulder level if possible).

Q: Is the step stool unsteady? If your loved one must use a step stool, get one with a bar to hold on to. Never use a chair as a step stool.

BATHROOMS: Look at all the bathrooms.

Q: Is the tub or shower floor slippery? Put a non-slip rubber mat or self-stick strips on the floor of the tub or shower.

Q: Does your loved one need some support when getting in and out of the tub or up from the toilet? Have a carpenter put grab bars inside the tub and next to the toilet.

BEDROOMS: Look at all the bedrooms.

Q: Is the light near the bed hard to reach? Place a lamp close to the bed where it's easy to reach.

Q: Is the path from the bed to the bathroom dark? Put in a nightlight so you can see where you're walking. Some nightlights go on by themselves after dark or you can buy nightlights with motion detectors that only go on when you're nearby.

Other Things You Can Do to Prevent Falls

- Encourage your loved one to exercise regularly. Exercise makes you stronger and improves balance and coordination.
- Have your loved one's doctor or pharmacist look at all the medications he or she takes, even over-the-counter medicines. Some can make you sleepy or dizzy. Advise your loved one to be particularly careful when walking around after taking those medicines.
- Have your loved one get regular vision checkups (at least once a year). Poor vision can increase the risk of falling.
- Have your loved one get up slowly after sitting or lying down.
- Be sure your loved one wears shoes both inside and outside the house and avoids going barefoot or wearing slippers.
- Improve the lighting in your loved one's home. Put in brighter light bulbs. Fluorescent bulbs are bright and cost less to use.
- It's safest to have uniform lighting in a room. Add lighting to dark areas. Hang lightweight curtains or shades to reduce glare.
- Paint a contrasting color on the top edge of all steps so you can see the stairs better. For example, use a light color paint on dark wood.

Here are a few other tips you can use to safe-proof your loved one's home:

- Keep emergency numbers in large print near each phone.
- Put a phone near the floor in case your loved one falls and can't get up.
- Think about having your loved one wear an alarm device that will bring help in case they've fallen and can't get up.

Fall Prevention in Dementia Patients: One Size Doesn't Fit All

Reducing falls for people with cognitive impairments like Dementia involves different approaches than for other people. A one-size-fits-all method of fall prevention isn't going to address each person's individual risk factors. No two people fall for exactly the same reason, and no prescribed set of interventions will work for everyone.

I came across a very interesting study that I wanted to share, as it presents some useful information. Researcher Fiona E. Shaw published her study in the July/August 2003 issue of *Geriatrics & Aging* estimating the annual incidence of falls in seniors with Dementia to be about 70-80 percent – that's almost double the incidence of falls for elderly people *without* Dementia. Additionally, nursing home residents with Dementia are three times more likely to sustain a fracture from a fall, and those who fracture a hip have a 50 percent higher mortality rate at one year than those without Dementia.

According to Ms. Shaw's study, a multifaceted intervention consisting of physiotherapy, environmental hazard reduction and cardiovascular interventions, including treatment of orthostatic hypotension (OH), a sudden drop in blood pressure, with Dementia patients who had fallen produced significant improvements in gait, environment and stability.

We use this study at *Homewatch CareGivers* to train our staff and family members to try other fall prevention techniques for people with Dementia, including the following:

1. **Consider a broad range of fall causes.** The person with Dementia may not be able to give a reliable history, and witnesses to falls may be unavailable. In the absence of hard facts, it's important to consider all the possible causes of a fall.

2. **Assess cognitively impaired people to determine the direction in which they are most likely to fall.** This will help you determine the body parts people are most likely to injure, so you can fit your loved one with protective padded clothing. People with Dementia tend to develop distinctive fall patterns, depending on the areas of the brain that are damaged and on muscular responses particular to the individual.

3. **Try soft, flexible moccasins or socks without shoes.** This type of footwear enables the cognitively impaired resident to feel the floor and compensate for declining depth perception, thereby reducing falls.

4. **Be on the lookout for OH.** A sudden drop in blood pressure is common in older people who have Dementia, but it is easily diagnosed and potentially treatable. Consider assessing the condition with continuous monitoring equipment, such as a noninvasive blood pressure monitor that constantly measures arterial blood pressure in the finger. This type of assessment is well tolerated and accurate.

5. **Small interventions can make big improvements in mobility.** Trying a different walking aid or finding more suitable shoes may make a big difference.

6. **Consider protective clothing.** Hip protectors, knee pads, elbow pads, wrist splints and soft foam helmets have shown great efficacy in reducing or eliminating serious injuries in people who fall.

7. **Nutrition changes.** Try supplementing the diets of people who have Dementia with calcium, vitamin D and vitamin C. These vitamins may help prevent fractures and reduce falls, according to several studies conducted in the United States and the United Kingdom.

Mr. and Mrs. Snyder: Alzheimer's Challenges with Falls

At *Homewatch Caregivers*, we care for a number of clients who have Alzheimer's disease. Mr. and Mrs. Snyder came into service with us about six months ago. Mrs. Snyder had Alzheimer's disease. I met Mr. Snyder (Jim) at a Rotary Club meeting in Michigan, where I was giving a presentation on fall prevention. After the meeting, Mr. Snyder approached me to talk about his wife. Mrs. Snyder (Alice) was 79 years old and was diagnosed with Alzheimer's disease officially five years ago. Mr. Snyder was 81 years old and his heart disease had progressed over the past year. He mentioned he felt weaker and was at the point where he needed help with his wife's care.

I made an appointment to complete an evaluation. The Snyders lived in a two-story house where all the bedrooms were upstairs. I immediately noted this as an area of concern. The Snyders had one daughter who lived in Orange County, California. My staff and I had a conference call with Mr. and Mrs. Snyder and their daughter Kim to determine what the family's goals were. While Kim was advocating that her parents move into an Assisted Living Community together, Mr. and Mrs. Snyder's wishes were to try to live as safely and independently as possible. They had been in their home for 41 years and truly didn't want to leave.

So the action plan I created for the Snyders was as follows:

1. I suggested the Snyders convert the downstairs den into the couple's bedroom and close off the upstairs to prevent any need for going up and down the stairs and to decrease the chances for a fall.
2. I proposed having a caregiver come into the house three hours in the morning and three hours in the evening, seven days a week to help care for Mrs. Snyder.
3. I created an additional plan that addressed Mrs. Snyder's Alzheimer's disease related to fall prevention.

The following is some specific information to consider related to falls and Alzheimer's disease. We used this approach with Mrs. Snyder.

As Alzheimer's disease progresses, keeping loved ones from falling can become increasingly difficult, in part because of the cognitive decline associated with Alzheimer's disease. For example, even though we explained to Mrs. Snyder that she shouldn't get up out of her chair or walk around without help, she continually tried to do these activities on her own because of her memory impairment. She's been walking when she needs to her whole life, so to remember now that she is not strong or steady enough to do this was a difficult change.

To address this issue, we trained Mr. Snyder on how to help his wife get in and out of chairs. We also strategically placed her walkers around the house. We also had the caregiver who was there in the mornings and evenings assist Mrs. Snyder with getting into and out of bed. We also took the following steps:

- **Visual Misperception:** Because Alzheimer's can affect visual-spatial abilities, a person can misinterpret what he/she sees and misjudge steps, uneven terrain, shiny areas on the floor or changes in floor color. We had Mrs. Snyder's vision checked regularly. In addition, we executed the fall prevention measures outlined in the section above.

- **Clutter:** Falls happen sometimes because of less than ideal home conditions, such as too much clutter to try to navigate around. Some people with Alzheimer's disease have a tendency to hoard things, which can increase the risk of tripping. This wasn't the case with the Snyder home, as it was a very well kept home.

- **Fatigue:** Some falls happen at a certain time of the day, such as in the evening before bed when your loved one is tired from the day. We addressed this issue by making sure a caregiver was there with Mrs. Snyder in the evening hours.

- **Medication Side Effects:** As we discussed earlier, some medications can increase the risk of falls. Antipsychotic medications, for example, can sometimes have a side effect of OH, where a person experiences a sudden drop in blood pressure when standing up too quickly. Other medications, such as hypnotics (medications that help facilitate sleep) can also cause lingering drowsiness that can increase the chance of falls. This was not an issue for Mrs. Snyder.

As of the writing of this book, the Snyders now have a live-in caregiver at their home around the clock. Both of their conditions declined to a point where they needed constant care. As the family evaluated this option versus the cost of a two-bedroom unit plus services at an Assisted Living Community, they discovered the in-home option was about the same cost ($8,400 per month), so chose to remain in their own home.

A Simple Checklist and Resources to Use

As I close this chapter, I want to summarize some of the key points and offer some simple tips to further help prevent devastating falls. As your loved one ages, physical changes and health conditions – and sometimes the medications used to treat those conditions – make falls more likely. We discussed this in detail throughout the chapter. We learned that falls are a leading cause of injury among older adults. Still, the fear of falling doesn't need to rule your loved one's or your life. Instead, consider six simple fall-prevention strategies:

1. **Make an appointment with your loved one's doctor.** Begin your fall-prevention plan by making an appointment with your loved one's doctor. Be prepared to answer questions such as:

   - **What medications is your loved one taking?** Make a list of all prescriptions and over-the-counter medications and supplements, or bring them with you to the appointment. The doctor can review these medications for side effects and interactions that may increase the risk of falling. To help with fall prevention, the doctor may consider weaning your loved one off certain medications, such as sedatives and some types of antidepressants.

   - **Has your loved one fallen before?** Write down the details, including when, where and how your loved one fell. Be prepared to discuss instances when your loved one almost fell but was caught by someone or managed to grab hold of something just in time. Details such as these may help your doctor identify specific fall-prevention strategies.

   - **Could your loved one's health conditions cause a fall?** Certain eye and ear disorders, heart/cardiovascular issues, diabetes or inflammatory conditions (arthritis) may increase the risk of falls. Be prepared to discuss your loved one's health conditions and how comfortable it is to walk and get around. For example, do they feel any dizziness, joint pain, numbness or shortness of breath when walking? The doctor may evaluate their muscle strength, balance and walking style (gait) as well.

2. **Keep 'em moving.** Physical activity can go a long way toward fall prevention. With the doctor's approval, consider low-impact exercise for your elder loved ones, such as walking, water workouts or Tai Chi – a gentle exercise that involves slow and graceful dance-like movements. Such activities reduce the risk of falls by improving strength, balance, coordination

and flexibility. If your loved one avoids physical activity because of a fear that a fall is more likely, tell the doctor. He or she may recommend carefully monitored exercise programs or refer your loved one to a physical therapist. The physical therapist can create a custom exercise program aimed at improving balance, flexibility, muscle strength and gait.

3. **Wear sensible shoes.** Sometimes all it takes to be more sure-footed and to prevent falls is a change in footwear. High heels, floppy slippers, flip flops and shoes with slick soles can make anyone slip, stumble and fall, and they need to go! Instead, make sure your loved one wears properly fitting, sturdy shoes with nonskid soles outside *and* inside the home.

4. **Remove home hazards.** Take a look around your loved one's home. The living room, kitchen, bedroom, bathroom, hallways and stairways may be filled with hazards. Please refer to the room-by-room list earlier in this chapter. Remember, to make your home safer:

   - Remove furniture, boxes, newspapers, electrical cords and phone cords from walkways.
   - Move coffee tables, magazine racks and plant stands from high-traffic areas.
   - Secure loose rugs with double-sided tape, tacks or a slip-resistant backing — or remove throw rugs entirely from the home.
   - Repair loose, wooden floor boards and ripped or damaged carpeting right away.
   - Store clothing, dishes, food and other necessities within easy reach on waist- to chest-high shelves.
   - Immediately clean spilled liquids, grease or food.
   - Use nonslip mats in the bathtub or shower.

5. **Light up their living space.** Keep your loved one's home brightly lit:

   - Place night lights in the bedrooms, bathrooms and hallways.
   - Place a lamp within reach of the bed for middle-of-the-night needs.

- Make sure the path is clear to light switches that aren't near room entrances. Consider trading traditional switches for glow-in-the-dark or illuminated switches.
- Turn on the lights before going up or down stairs.
- Store flashlights in easy-to-find places in case of power outages.

6. **Use assistive devices.** The doctor might recommend that your loved one use a cane or walker to keep steady. Other assistive devices can help, too. For example:

  - Hand rails for both sides of stairways;
  - Nonslip treads for bare-wood steps;
  - A raised toilet seat or one with armrests;
  - Grab bars for the shower, tub and toilet;
  - A sturdy plastic seat for the shower or tub — plus a hand-held shower nozzle for bathing while sitting down.

A Set of Resources for You

The following are some online resources that you can print out and use in your home and/or give to your loved ones:

- Homewatch CareGivers *Fall Prevention Guide*: **www.businesswire.com/ news/home/20130918005975/en/Homewatch-CareGivers-releases-falls-prevention-guide-living#.VM605-85DIU**
- Fall Prevention Resource Guide: **www.tompkins-co.org/cofa/ Services/documents/2013-March30FallPreventionResourceGuide-onlinerevisiononly.pdf**
- Fall Prevention Tips: **www.activeforever.com/fall-prevention**

CHAPTER 5

The Gift of Hospice

I am ashamed to say that both my mother and father died without the gift of hospice.

I am ashamed of this because both my parents were eligible for hospice under Medicare guidelines and we did not access this valued resource. Further, I work as a hospice professional and should have known better. My mom and dad, as well as my brother and I, could have benefited greatly from the gift of hospice.

Hospice is one of the best-kept secrets that can make an end-of-life journey more peaceful, as opposed to filled with drama and pain. As I wrote about in Chapter One, it's hard to be both a caregiver and a loved one. In retrospect, it was so obvious that my parents could have benefited from hospice. Instead, because I was trying to be a loved one and caregiver at the same time, their needs went right over my head. So again, I wonder how people with no healthcare experience deal with such challenges.

This chapter will help you understand better how hospice and palliative care can help you and your family members de-mystify all the false assumptions around hospice and how to select the best hospice for you and your loved one.

Mom and Dad: How They Missed the Gift of Hospice

After Dad's stroke, his health declined rapidly. He lost weight; his abilities to complete activities of daily living diminished; and his difficulty with swallowing led to respiratory issues. Dad was clearly a good candidate for hospice care. Sadly, Dad was in a nursing home and died alone. I keep going over and over in my mind how I could have made his last months with us better … how I could have enhanced his quality of life. With hospice, he would have been much more comfortable and the chances of him dying alone would have been reduced. The skilled nursing facility he was in should have suggested to our family to consider hospice, but they didn't. More importantly, I should have seen this and requested a hospice consultation. Neither of these things occurred, and as a result, Dad died without the gift of hospice.

Many years later after my mother's fall, she progressively declined; another sign that we should have asked for a hospice consult. I knew that anyone could call a hospice and ask for a professional to come out and talk with them about their options. I should have done this, but didn't. As I look back on the last year of my mother's life, it's now clearer than ever I made a big mistake by not having a hospice professional come out and talk with me, my brother and mother. While we had a caregiver with my mother whenever my brother was at work, the support of a hospice company would have made a significant difference. Mom was eligible to access her hospice benefit long before she died but she didn't. I should have recognized this and helped her receive the gift of hospice. Mom met the hospice eligibility requirements because she was losing weight, she experienced more frequent Urinary Tract Infections, had severe loss of mobility and mild Dementia.

My BIG lesson learned from these experiences: I should have asked for a hospice professional to talk with my family about what they could offer.

In my research, I found that the National Hospice and Palliative Care Association completed several studies, asking family members about their hospice experience. One thing that almost every family member said was, "I wish I would have accessed my loved one's hospice benefit sooner than we did." I wish I would have for my mom and dad. Period. I hope what you learn here will prevent you from experiencing the same regret I've had.

What Services Does Hospice Provide?

The term "hospice" (from the same linguistic root as "hospitality") can be traced back to medieval times, when it referred to a place of shelter and rest for weary or ill travelers on a long journey. The name was first applied to specialized care for dying patients by Dame Cicely Saunders, M.D., who began her work with the terminally ill in 1948 and eventually went on to create the first modern hospice – St. Christopher's Hospice – in a residential suburb of London. We discuss Dr. Saunders' contributions later in the chapter.

Hospice is *not* a place but a specialized approach to care. Hospice is a philosophy of healthcare focused on providing comfort care to terminally ill patients. This type of care is also called palliative care by the medical community. Hospice care is a specialized type of clinical care that helps alleviate pain and suffering for the patient who is near the end of his or her life. Hospice also provides emotional support to the patient's family. Ninety-five percent of hospice care is provided in the patient's home (including assisted living, independent and skilled senior living communities). The other 5 percent is delivered in a hospital setting or in an Inpatient Hospice Unit (IPU).

I think the creation of the Medicare Hospice Benefit was one of the best things our government ever did. U.S. Senator Bob Dole (R-KS) was a champion of the legislation that launched the benefit in 1986, when states were given the option of including hospice in their Medicaid programs. Hospice care also was made available to terminally ill nursing home residents at this time. By 1993, President Clinton included hospice as a nationally guaranteed benefit and hospice became an accepted part of end-of-life care in the United States.

The section below will outline the history of hospice. The Medicare Hospice legislation called out a set of rules called Conditions of Participation (CoPs). All hospice providers are mandated to follow these CoPs, which lay the framework for the services provided.

Hospice is not a place but a specialized approach to care, providing comfort or palliative care to terminally ill patients.

Here is how a hospice team works: Through conversations about the patient's care, including his or her goals and wishes, the hospice works with the patient, family and attending doctor to develop a plan of care that is focused on helping the patient find comfort and peace. Hospice uses a holistic approach, focused on improving the clinical, emotional and spiritual conditions of patients, as well as their loved ones.

Hospice Interdisciplinary Care Team

The hospice interdisciplinary care team is central to the hospice care philosophy. This group of specialists – including hospice physicians, nurse case managers, nursing aides, social workers, chaplains, trained volunteers and bereavement coordinators – offers emotional, spiritual and clinical support to reduce suffering for patients and their families.

The team meets weekly to ensure the care plan provides the best possible care to the patient and loved ones based on their current needs. Members of the team are available by phone all day and every day, should a need or question arise.

Four Levels of Hospice Care

Every hospice offers four different levels of care to meet the needs of the patient and family, as determined in collaboration with the interdisciplinary care team. The levels of care as outlined in the CoPs are:

1. **Routine home care:** Routine home care is standard care given in the patient's place of residence and provided by the interdisciplinary team, including physicians, nurses, certified nursing aides, chaplains, social workers and trained volunteers. There is no time limit to this type of hospice care. Routine home hospice care will be provided as long as it is believed that the patient will continue to benefit clinically. This usually consists of a weekly visit by a nurse and two or three visits by a home health aide per week. A social worker can assist the family, should they need the care that this professional provides. If the family so desires, a spiritual care member of the team (chaplain) can visit and assist as well. Every hospice maintains a trained group of volunteers who can assist the patient and family in a number of ways, such as visiting with the patient to provide companionship, running errands or doing other tasks.

2. **Respite care:** This level of care is designed to give the caregiver a period of rest. Providing care for a terminally ill loved one can be exhausting. With respite care, the patient typically goes to an IPU for a five-day stay, during which time the caregiver can relax and take some time for himself or herself.

3. **Continuous care:** Providing comfort for the patient is critical. Each patient's care is reviewed periodically and sometimes an added level of nursing care is required. Continuous care was developed for exactly that. Hospices offer continuous care at the patient's residence during a short-term, temporary crisis when there is a need for constant skilled nursing. This type of care is only provided in the most critical of cases, maintaining a focus on hospice care.

4. **General inpatient care:** Typically, this is a brief period of inpatient care in a clinical setting with a 24-hour nursing staff that helps to manage acute symptoms. It may be required for procedures that necessitate a higher level of nursing care to manage the pain or symptoms. Hospice providers partner with many hospitals and

medical facilities within their communities, so if the need for general inpatient care arises, a convenient location is at hand. The typical inpatient stay is five days. When the crisis has passed, the patient is returned to the routine level of care wherever the patient calls home.

Who Pays for Hospice Care?

Hospice care is paid for by Medicare, Medicaid in most states, the Department of Veterans Affairs (VA), most private insurance plans, HMOs and other managed care organizations.

Home hospice care usually costs less than care in hospitals, nursing homes or other institutional settings. This is because hospice uses less high-cost technology than a hospital or inpatient setting, and the hospice staff, family and volunteers provide most of the care, rather than physicians, nurses and other medical professionals.

To receive payment from Medicare, the hospice must be approved by Medicare to provide hospice services. In this case, the patient and family pay nothing for hospice care, but you may have co-payments for certain prescriptions.

To qualify for the Medicare hospice benefit, a doctor and the hospice medical director (also a doctor) must examine the patient and certify that the patient meets eligibility to access their hospice benefits. The hospice benefit starts with two periods of 90 days each; then an unlimited number of 60-day periods. A doctor or nurse practitioner must re-certify the patient in a face-to-face visit before the third election period, and then again before each benefit period after that. This means that the patient must be seen by his or her own doctor or the hospice doctor to be certified for the first 180 days of hospice care. After the first 180 days, the patient must be seen again to be re-certified every 60 days for as long as the patient is getting hospice care.

The patient signs a statement that says he or she understands the nature of the illness and hospice care, and that he or she wants to be admitted to hospice. By signing the statement, the patient chooses the Medicare Hospice Benefit for all care related to his or her illness or condition. A family member may sign the statement if the patient is unable to do so.

If you're not sure how hospice might work for you, Medicare offers a free, one-time-only hospice consultation. You can meet with a hospice medical director or hospice doctor to discuss your care options and treatment needs. You don't have to choose hospice care if you use this consultation service.

Medicaid Coverage

Most states have a Medicaid Hospice Benefit, which is patterned after the Medicare Hospice Benefit. To receive the Medicaid benefit, all other private funds and insurance coverage must be exhausted first.

Private Insurance

Most private health insurance companies include hospice care as a benefit. Be sure to ask about your insurance coverage, not only for hospice, but also for personal home health care.

Private Pay

If insurance coverage is not available or does not cover all the costs of hospice, the patient and the family can hire hospice providers and pay for services out of pocket. Some hospices are able to provide services without charge if a patient has limited or no financial resources.

A Story I Hope You Can Learn From

I'm embarrassed to even share this story, as I have been a strong hospice advocate and healthcare professional for over 17 years. I mention it as a cautionary tale, so you don't make the same mistake.

My personal home care company, *Homewatch CareGivers*, was working with a man, Jack, age 70, who was caring for his elderly mother, Ellie, age 92, who lived in his home. The mother had cardiac issues and advancing Alzheimer's disease. Jack was a loving, kind caregiver to his mother. We provided a caregiver to come help the son out and give him a break each week.

While I was visiting one day, I had a nice talk with Jack about end-of-life care for his mother. He shared with me that his wife had died of breast cancer and was in hospice at the end. He told me he had a positive experience with hospice and still donated to one particular hospice. Jack asked if I could start the process with that hospice for a referral for his mother.

I agreed and called the hospice's in-take department and told them that the family would like someone from the hospice to come out for a talk and see Ellie. The woman in the in-take department told me they needed a physician order before they could come out to speak to anyone. I paused in amazement. I explained that the son just wanted a visit and to talk with someone. She refused. I was shocked! I asked to talk with the clinical director. He wasn't available. I asked to speak with a supervisor. No one was available to help me give this hospice a referral. I finally said I would like to leave a message for the clinical director, which I did. I hung up the phone and started shaking my head.

Two days passed and I never received a call back. I called again and asked to speak with the clinical director. No luck, so I left another message for the clinical director, explaining the situation and asking for a call back. Two more days went by, and I still had no word from them!

I called Jack and politely explained what I experienced and I made a suggestion to contact another hospice. He said he wanted this hospice because of his wife. I respected my client's wishes and told him I would forge on.

That day, I called the hospice's CEO, and after a 15-minute wait, was finally able to talk with her and explain that I was seeking a visit from her hospice to my client. She assured me that she would handle everything.

I called Jack two days later, and he told me that he did receive a call from the hospice right away but that the hospice couldn't make a visit until they received an order from his mother's physician. He said he spent the next two days trying to connect with his mother's physician, which he was finally able to do.

This specific type of hospice not only makes it difficult for people to obtain hospice care but is NOT what you should expect when you call a hospice for help. I am still in total shock that this hospice wouldn't send someone out to talk with the son immediately. This lack of compassion and frigid behavior prolonged the son and his mother from getting the care and support they needed. It also caused me to **never, ever** use this hospice again. You **DO NOT** need a physician's order to talk with anyone about hospice, and yet this hospice chose to create barriers that do not need to be there.

This is an example of a hospice **I WOULD NOT USE**. Not only because you don't need a physician order to speak to them, but also because of the two messages left with no return call from the clinical director and the long wait time in getting to the CEO, who didn't eliminate the barrier, but instead reinforced it.

I'm still shocked! I assure you, there are many wonderful hospice companies all across the country who would never think of doing such a thing!

Later in this chapter, I discuss what you should look for when considering a hospice. Let me stress again that you do not need a physician order to have a hospice come talk with you. You do need a physician's order when you select to have your loved ones access their hospice benefits.

A Short History of Hospice

To truly understand the value of the gift of hospice and how hospice can assist you and a loved one dealing with a life-challenging illness, it's important to understand how hospice developed in our country and around the world. The U.S. model of medicine is rooted in curative medicine. While we are blessed to have one of the best medical (not health) models of care in the world, it sometimes can be a little over the top. Futile care is a term used to describe when curative medicine turns "ugly," with physicians poking, cutting and prescribing this, that and the other thing with truly no hope of curing the patient. There is a saying used amongst the medical community that defines futile care in a tongue-in-cheek way. "Do you know why they put nails in a coffin? To prevent the oncologist from giving the last dose of chemo!"

Palliative care is a medical discipline focused on pain and symptom management and keeping a patient comfortable when a terminal illness has taken hold of a patient. Hospice is the practice of palliative care for patients dealing with a challenging illness that threatens life.

Many societies throughout history had special ways of caring for the dying and the bereaved. For example, in ancient China, "death houses" offered a place for the destitute to stay when they were dying. In New Zealand, Maori customs gave practical support for the family at the time of death, and encouraged the community to participate in mourning rituals. Wise elders in East Africa gave both practical and spiritual support to the dying and bereaved.

In Western Europe and North America, until the 19th century, caring for the dying and the bereaved was seen primarily as the job of the family and the church. In the last 100 years, dying has increasingly been viewed as a medical event, not as a milestone in the life and history of a family.

More than 4,000 local hospice and palliative care programs in the United States offer specialized care to people suffering from fatal illnesses, such as cancer and renal failure. Good hospices are rooted in, and responsive to, the communities they serve, and to the people who live and die there.

The Hospice Timeline: From the Middle Ages to the 21st Century

To give you some perspective, the following is a brief overview of hospice and palliative care around the world throughout the ages:

During the Middle Ages, religious orders in Europe established "hospices" at key crossroads on the way to religious shrines, like Santiago de Compostela, Chartres and Rome. These shelters helped pilgrims, many of whom were traveling to these shrines seeking miraculous cures of chronic and fatal illnesses, and many of whom died while on their pilgrimages.

From the 16th to 18th centuries, religious orders offered care for the sick and dying in locally or regionally based institutions (church-run hospitals). However, most people died at home, cared for by the women in the family.

By the 1800s, Madame Garnier of Lyon, France, opened a "calvaire" to care for the dying.

In 1879, Mother Mary Aikenhead of the Irish Sisters of Charity opened Our Lady's Hospice in Dublin, caring only for the dying.

By the late 19th century, the increase in municipal or charitably-financed infirmaries, almshouses and hospitals, and the expansion of medical knowledge, started the process of "medicalizing" dying. (By the mid-20th century, almost 80 percent of the people in the United States died in a hospital or nursing home.)

In 1905, the Irish Sisters of Charity opened St. Joseph's Hospice in East London to care for the sick and the dying.

Also in the early 1900s in London, St. Luke's Hospice and the Hospice of God opened to serve the dying poor.

From 1935 to the 1990s, interest grew in the psychosocial aspects of dying and bereavement, sparked by the work of Worcester, Bowlby, Lindemann, Hinton, Parkes, Kubler-Ross, Raphael, Worden and others.

From 1957 to 1967, Cicely Saunders, a young physician previously trained as a nurse and a social worker, worked at St. Joseph's Hospice, studying pain control in advanced cancer cases. Dr. Saunders pioneered in the regular use of opioid analgesics given "by the clock" instead of waiting for the pain to return before giving drugs. This is now standard practice in good hospice and palliative care. Cicely Saunders is considered the modern founder of hospice.

In 1967, Dr. Saunders opened St. Christopher's Hospice in London, emphasizing the multi-disciplinary approach to caring for the dying, the regular use of opioids to control physical pain, and careful attention to social, spiritual and psychological suffering in patients and families.

From 1968 to 1975, many hospice and palliative care programs opened in Great Britain, adapting the St. Christopher's model to local needs, offering inpatient and home care.

In 1974, New Haven Hospice (now known as Connecticut Hospice) began hospice home care in the United States, caring for people with cancer, ALS and other fatal illnesses. Florence Wald, along with two pediatricians and a chaplain, founded this hospice – the first to open in the nation.

Also in 1974, the first hospice legislation was introduced by Senators Frank Church and Frank E. Moss to provide federal funds for hospice programs. The legislation was not enacted.

From 1974 to 1978, hospices and palliative care units opened across North America. These included Hospice of Marin in California, the Palliative Care Unit at the Royal Victoria Hospital in Montreal, the Support Team at St. Luke's Hospital in New York City, and Church Hospital Hospice in Baltimore.

In 1978, a U.S. Department of Health, Education and Welfare task force reported, "The hospice movement as a concept for the care of the terminally ill and their families is a viable concept and one which holds out a means of providing more humane care for Americans dying of terminal illness while possibly reducing costs. As such, it is the proper subject of federal support."

By 1979, the Health Care Financing Administration (HCFA) initiated demonstration programs at 26 hospices across the country to assess the cost effectiveness of hospice care and to help determine what a hospice is and what it should provide. One of those hospices was right here in my home state of Michigan.

In 1980, the W.K. Kellogg Foundation awarded a grant to the Joint Commission on Accreditation of Hospitals (JCAHO) to investigate the status of hospices and to develop standards for hospice accreditation.

By the 1980s, hospice care, usually emphasizing home care, expanded throughout the United States. Medicare added a hospice benefit in 1986. Hospices began to care for people with advanced AIDS, and by the end of that decade all patients with a terminal illness who met eligible guidelines could access their hospice benefits and receive the gift of hospice.

In 1982, Congress included a provision to create a Medicare Hospice Benefit in the Tax Equity and Fiscal Responsibility Act of 1982, with a 1986 sunset provision.

In 1984, JCAHO initiated hospice accreditation.

In 1986, the Medicare Hospice Benefit is made permanent by the U.S. Congress and hospices are given a 10 percent increase in reimbursement rates. States received the option of including hospice in their Medicaid programs and hospice care was now available to terminally ill nursing home residents. This act "turbo-charged" the growth of hospice in the United States.

By the end of the decade, the Government Accounting Office released a study stating that only about 35 percent of eligible hospices are Medicare-certified. There are several reasons listed, including the low payment rates HCFA had established for hospices. In 1989, Congress gave hospices their first increase in reimbursement since 1986 (20 percent) and tied future increases to the annual increase in the hospital market basket through a provision contained in the Omnibus Budget Reconciliation Act of 1989.

From 1990 to 2000, more than 3,000 hospices and palliative care programs served the United States. There also were well-established hospice and palliative care companies in Canada, Australia, New Zealand, and much of Asia and Western Europe. By the year 2000, hospice and palliative care was available in over 40 countries worldwide, including many less-developed nations.

Also during the 1990s, the World Health Organization set standards for palliative care and pain control, calling it a "priority." But studies showed that most patients still received little or no effective palliative care, and pain was often very poorly controlled, primarily due to a lack of medical knowledge, to unfounded fears of addiction, and, in less-developed nations, to a shortage of opioids (effective pain medication).

In 1991, the Commission on the Future Structure of Veterans Health Care (Mission Commission) released a report recommending the inclusion of hospice care in veterans' benefit packages.

In 1992, Congress passed the Indian Health Care Improvement Act, calling for a hospice feasibility study.

In 1993, hospice was included as a nationally guaranteed benefit under President Clinton's health care reform proposal. By this point, hospice was an accepted part of the health care continuum.

During 1994, HCFA sent a memo alerting the regions of problems regarding questionable certifications and re-certifications of terminal illnesses. This results in the first "focused medical review" for hospices and a wake-up call to the industry to improve its documentation and certification procedures or be denied payments. Hospice was starting to become big business in the United States.

In 1995, HCFA released an expanded version of the Hospice Interpretive Guidelines, which provided much-needed clarification of the Conditions of Participation (CoP). The Civilian Health and Medical Program of the Uniformed Services (CHAMPUS) Hospice Benefit was implemented June 1, 1995. This program mirrored the Medicare Hospice Benefit in CoPs and reimbursement.

By the 21st century, the principles of good hospice and palliative care are understood and accepted, and all patients with advanced illness, and their families, are assured of competent and compassionate care in their homes, in nursing homes and in hospitals across the United States.

Hospice Enters the Public Consciousness

One of the defining events that brought hospice to the consciousness of America was a book based on more than 500 interviews with dying patients entitled, *On Death and Dying*. Written by Dr. Elisabeth Kubler-Ross, the book identifies the five stages through which many terminally ill patients progress. The book became an international bestseller. Within it, Dr. Kubler-Ross makes a plea for home care as opposed to treatment in an institutional setting, and argues that patients should have a choice and the ability to participate in the decisions that affect their destiny.

In 1972, Dr. Kubler-Ross testified at the first national hearings on the subject of death with dignity, conducted by the U.S. Senate Special Committee on Aging. In her testimony, Kubler-Ross states, "We live in a very particular death-denying society. We isolate both the dying and the old, and it serves a purpose. They are reminders of our own mortality. We should not institutionalize people. We can give families more help with home care and visiting nurses, giving the families and the patients the spiritual, emotional and financial help in order to facilitate the final care at home."

All of the events mentioned in the hospice timeline above gave us hospice as we know it today. In essence, we are all paying for hospice through our taxes, which is another good reason to take advantage of this wonderful gift.

Hospice Myths

It's only natural that we fear what we don't understand. This is one of the main reasons people don't elect to access their hospice benefit. There are many, many myths surrounding hospice. The following are some of the common myths and what the truth really is.

Myth: "I thought that if my mother was under the care of hospice, she could no longer go to the hospital if she needed to. In the past year, she has been hospitalized several times because her pain got out of control."

Truth: While hospice strives to manage pain and other uncomfortable symptoms outside of the hospital setting, a hospice patient always has the choice of whether or not to go to the hospital. The Medicare Hospice Benefit covers short-term general inpatient care in the hospital when a patient's symptoms can no longer be managed in another care setting.

Myth: "I always thought that "hospice" was a place – you know, that building that I pass on the way home from work."

Truth: Hospice is a philosophy of care, not a place.

Myth: "Hospice is only for elderly people."

Truth: Hospice is for anyone with a terminal illness with a diagnosis of six months or less of life. In fact, there are several hospices that specialize in caring for terminally ill children.

Myth: "Hospice is for people who don't need a high level of care."

Truth: Hospice is serious medical care and requires experienced medical and nursing professionals with skills in symptom control. Hospice offers state-of-the-art palliative care, using advanced technologies to prevent or alleviate distressing symptoms. One level of hospice care is called the General Inpatient (GIP) level of care and is considered the "ICU of Hospice."

Myth: "The patient can't keep his or her own doctor."

Truth: The patient may choose to keep his or her own doctor or choose the hospice's medical director. The patient and family can decide what is best.

Myth: "Hospice can't help take care of my dad because he's residing in an assisted living apartment."

Truth: Hospice provides care wherever a patient calls home, including, but not limited to assisted living facilities, skilled nursing facilities, independent living facilities and personal homes.

Myth: "The doctor said I had to sign a 'Do Not Resuscitate' (DNR) order for my wife in order for her to get hospice. I just couldn't do that; it seemed so final."

Truth: A patient can receive hospice without having signed a DNR. The hospice regulation actually says that hospices cannot discriminate against patients because of any advance directive choices.

Myth: "I didn't consider hospice care early enough because my dad was still getting blood transfusions regularly. We weren't ready to stop because each time he would get one, it seemed to make him feel better for a few days. We just wanted him to feel like himself for as long as possible."

Truth: The Medicare Hospice Benefit may cover chemotherapy, radiation, blood transfusions or other treatments if those treatments are providing comfort for patients eligible to receive the benefit (having a life expectancy of six months or less if the illness runs its normal course).

Myth: "I thought that hospice was only for patients with cancer. I didn't realize that my husband who suffered from Alzheimer's disease could have benefited from support from the hospice caregiving team, too."

Truth: More than 50 percent of hospice patients nationwide have diagnoses other than cancer. Many hospice patients are diagnosed with advanced stages of chronic diseases, like pulmonary disease, Alzheimer's disease, renal disease, HIV/AIDS and cardiovascular or neuromuscular diseases.

Myth: "I was under the impression that I had to be available as the designated caregiver 24 hours a day in order for my mom to get hospice."

Truth: Some hospices do require caregivers to be in place prior to the patient being admitted, but this is NOT true under the hospice benefit guidelines. Many hospices can coordinate community resources to keep the patient at home for as long as possible, and then help the patient find an alternative location to receive care when care at home is no longer possible.

Myth: "My dad lives at home. We weren't considering hospice for him because we thought it was too expensive. Between the doctor's visits and the cost of medications today, we have to save everything we can to make sure we can care for his ongoing needs."

Truth: The Medicare and Medicaid Hospice benefits cover services at 100 percent, so there is no cost to the patient. If patients have private insurance or managed care, hospices will assist in checking their benefit coverage to make sure patients and families understand any potential out-of-pocket costs.

Myth: "I wanted to learn more about hospice, but thought I had to wait for the doctor to bring it up first, so he could order it for my brother."

Truth: Patients and their families can choose to talk with a hospice anytime. You DO NOT need to have a physician order to have a consultation to discuss the benefit of hospice at any time. Hospices, however, cannot provide hands-on care to a patient without a physician's order. Hospices will work with each patient's physician to identify the patient's individual needs.

Myth: "I was so scared to even say 'hospice.' I thought it meant I had to give up. Give up hope. Give up trying. Give up praying for a cure."

Truth: In order to receive hospice, the patient must be eligible and have an understanding that hospice focuses on comfort care (palliative), not a cure. But patients and families do not have to be "ready to die" before getting the care they need and deserve. Hospice helps patients and families deal with what is happening to them on their own terms and in their own time frame. It is important to get hospice early, so that the benefit can help patients prepare and get ready for what is happening; it is not required that patients be ready prior to receiving care.

Myth: "Hospice is only for patients who are close to death or actively dying."

Truth: If there is one myth that bothers me most, it's this one. Because of the highly skilled care that hospice workers provide to their patients, hospice works best when the team has time to deliver it. The dying process takes time. Patients and their loved ones need medical care, as well as information and support. Social workers and chaplains need time to work with patients and their loved ones to bring them to a place of acceptance. Nurses and doctors need time to get the patient's symptoms optimally managed.

The work of the dying takes more time than the average length a patient is on hospice. Currently, the average length of stay in hospice care is only 14-20 days. It saddens me to think of all the care those patients missed out on.

Removing the stigma of hospice and redefining end-of-life care is essential to the future of health care. The population of seniors in the United States is expected to double in the next 30 years. That means more people will be living with chronic, life-limiting illness and will need expert end-of-life care. Dispelling these myths about hospice can bring us one step closer to providing quality, highly skilled care to patients at the end of life.

The truth is, hospice enriches life in many surprising ways.

Rose's Journey

Rose was an 88-year-old woman whom my company, *Homewatch CareGivers*, was caring for in a very nice senior assisted living community. Her niece lived in Florida and oversaw Rose's care. *Homewatch CareGivers* provided personal care services for Rose three times a week for three hours a day. Rose suffered from chronic lung disease and had slight Dementia. She was a delight to care for and it was an honor and privilege to know Rose personally.

One day, I received a call from Rose's niece, Arlene. Arlene told me that she received a call from the assisted living center saying that Rose had declined and needed more care and supervision than the facility could provide. They said that Rose would need to move out. Arlene was devastated and asked for our help to find out how to keep Rose where she was at. I told Arlene that we would make a visit the next day to see what we could do.

So the following day, the *Homewatch* nurse and I visited Rose. She had, in fact, declined since I last saw her two months earlier. Her Dementia had advanced and she was showing signs of edema in both legs, with a sore developing on her left leg. I could understand why the assisted living center had called Arlene.

The first thing we did was contact Rose's physician, who happened to have one of his nurse practitioners in the building at that moment. She was able to stop by and see Rose while we were there. Based on my prior hospice experience, I was sure Rose was eligible to access her hospice benefit, and I knew we could come up with a workable solution. The following was the plan we developed, along with her physician and niece, to keep Rose safe and secure in the assisted living center.

Care Plan for Rose

1. We recommended having a hospice that we worked with come out to complete an evaluation of Rose. If Rose was indeed eligible, hospice care would begin right away.
2. Rose was in need of 24-hour care because of her Dementia, which put her at risk for wandering. We proposed having caregivers from my company stay with Rose around the clock at the assisted living center.
3. We also created a schedule where our nurse from *Homewatch* would make more frequent visits to see Rose to assess any other changes in her condition.

I called Arlene when I got back to the office and shared our recommendations, which Arlene agreed to. I then called the hospice we worked with to make a referral. They sent a nurse out the next day to evaluate Rose's eligibility to elect her hospice benefit. Rose did meet eligibility for services, which started for her the same day. The hospice created a plan of care that they coordinated with *Homewatch*. We were able to find two caregivers that shared a schedule of providing 24-hour, live-in care.

Rose was made comfortable and she stayed safe in her unit at the assisted living center. During the next eight months, we cared for Rose along with the hospice interdisciplinary team. Rose's condition started to decline further, and she was recertified for a second period of hospice care. I stayed in close contact with Arlene, so she knew what was occurring.

About a month later, we received a call from hospice saying that Rose was experiencing some break-through pain and her symptoms were not managed to the degree they would like. The hospice and I called Arlene together and we recommended that Rose be admitted to the hospice's Inpatient Hospice Unit (IPU) to receive more intensive care to get her pain and symptoms under control. Arlene approved the decision and Rose was admitted to the IPU. As I mentioned earlier, the GIP level of care is intended to be a short-term stay (usually five or six days in the IPU). That was the last time I saw Rose, as she ended up passing away in the IPU.

Selecting the Right Hospice

Many families I work with ask me, "What should I look for when selecting a hospice?"

I always reply, "All hospices are NOT equal!"

The Diane Rehm show on National Public Radio (NPR) recently held a panel discussion reacting to a *Washington Post* article, entitled, "Dying and Profit: the Evolution of Hospice." (http://wapo.st/1CZiHGc)

The article basically said that for-profit hospices offer sub-par care. Both the article and NPR panel, in my humble opinion, were misleading and didn't address the true issue, which is what do consumers need to know in selecting the best hospice for themselves or their loved ones?

I have worked for both types of hospice companies, and to be completely honest, there are good and bad in both. The big claim in the *Washington Post* article is that for-profit hospices skimp on nursing visits. I have never found that to be the case. In addition, there are some not-for-profit hospices that act more like fund-development companies than hospice providers. So, I urge you to investigate the hospice thoroughly and know what criteria is most important when selecting a hospice to care for yourself or a loved one.

Here are a few questions that every customer should ask a prospective hospice:

- What is your turnover rate in your organization? The national average is 15 percent for hospice companies. If the company you are speaking to has a higher turnover rate, you need to ask why!
- What is the average caseload for your nurses? The national average is 13 patients per nurse. Obviously this number is going to fluctuate based on the hospice's census. This is a KEY question to ask and understand.
- Are your physicians board-certified in hospice and palliative care medicine? Just like you won't go to a family practice physician for open-heart surgery (you'd want a board-certified cardiovascular surgeon), you want a physician who is board-certified in hospice and palliative care medicine on the hospice company team you select.
- Does the hospice have full-time physicians on staff? You want to know if the hospice you select has a full-time medical director.
- Does the hospice offer all four levels of hospice care? There are four levels of hospice care that we learned about earlier: Routine, Respite, Continuous Care and General Inpatient (GIP). You want to make certain the hospice you select offers all four levels. Ask for details in how they offer these levels of care as well. In particular, the GIP level of care is the "ICU" of hospice care and is intended to care for patients who have break-through pain and symptom management issues. You need to know and understand how the hospice you select delivers this level of care should your loved one ever need it.
- Does the hospice offer music therapy? The basic hospice benefit does not require a hospice to offer music therapy. If the hospice you select offers music therapy, they are far beyond what the basic hospice benefit requires!
- How many volunteers does the hospice have? The use of volunteers is part of the CoPs a licensed hospice must offer. Ask how many volunteers the hospice has and how many volunteer hours the hospice provides per month.

These are just a few questions that will help guide you in selecting the best hospice for your loved one and you. It is NOT an issue of for-profit vs. not-for-profit but rather which hospice company offers the most outstanding care. You, as a consumer, need to know what makes a hospice excellent, good, bad or just so-so. The answer to these questions will help guide you in your interview process as you select a hospice.

Helpful Hospice Resources

Here are a set of online resources that will help you further understand how to give your loved one the gift of hospice:

- National Hospice and Palliative Care Organization: **www.nhpco.org**
- Hospice Net: **hospicenet.org**
- Hospice and Palliative Care Center: **hospicecarecenter.org/content/ resources**
- International Association for Hospice and Palliative Care: **www.hospicecare.com/resources**
- Hospice Foundation of America: **hospicefoundation.org**
- Seasons Hospice and Palliative Care: **www.seasons.org**

CHAPTER 6

100+ Helpful Tips and Tools to Help Your Parents Age with Dignity and Grace

Throughout my journey of taking care of my mom and dad, I have gathered many useful resources and pieces of information that I would like to pass along to you. The following are more than 100 helpful tips, tools and resources to help you on your journey of taking care of *your* loved ones.

- The *Homewatch CareGivers* website, **www.thehomecareexpert.com**, holds many useful pieces of information and resources for you on a variety of topics. I write a weekly blog with a video that also gives many helpful tips. Go to the **Resources** section of the website and click on **Blog**.

- Dehydration can cause dementia-like symptoms and accelerate heat stroke. The Centers for Disease Control recommends drinking cool, nonalcoholic beverages to prevent dehydration. For those people like my mother, who do not like drinking fluids, fruits like watermelon can provide a great source of hydration.

- If you're seeking to hire a professional caregiving company, make sure you ask if the company completes a national criminal background check, as well as a motor vehicle background review on all of their caregivers. NEVER, NEVER, EVER hire a company that does not do these two things. Furthermore, the background checks need to be repeated every six months, as things change.

- Make sure the caregiving company you hire completes regular quality assurance checks. These spot checks on the caregiver should be done by one of the company's professional staff members to make sure all is well in the home and that the care plan is being followed.

- Many families ask, "When is the right time to use hospice for a loved one?" The answer is sooner than later. In a recent survey, 98 percent of the families interviewed said, "I wish I would have started hospice sooner!"

- Check out **www.Caring.com** – an excellent website to help you learn about community resources when caring for loved ones.

- Call your local health department and ask to talk to a public health nurse about your concerns. This nurse will help you identify resources in your community.

- Consult an elder law attorney with any legal issues that may arise. You can locate an elder law attorney near you at: **www.elderlawanswers.com/elder-law-attorneys**.

- If your loved one is a veteran, there is a little known benefit offered by the Department of Veteran's Affairs (VA) called "Aid and Attendance." This benefit helps pay for personal in-home healthcare.

You can become more familiar with it at: **www.americanveteransaid. com/landing/lp_2/aid_and_attendance_2.html**.

- Each state has an agency called the Area Agency on Aging 1-b. These agencies provide a wealth of information. You can start at: **www.aaa1b.org**.

- There are typically four ways to pay for personal care home health services, including private pay, insurance (private and/or long-term care), the VA's Aid and Attendance benefit or tapping into your home's equity/mortgage. Check your loved one's insurance policies to see if they might help pay for in-home care.

- If your older loved ones enjoy using a computer, here is a resource just for them: **www.mygait.com**.

- A Place for Mom (**www.aplaceformom.com**) is a company that can help you locate the care you need for your loved one, whether it's in-home care or a senior living facility.

- To find a hospice that's right for you and your loved one, you can start at the National Hospice and Palliative Care Organization: **www.nhpco.org**.

- To find a Geriatric Case Manager to help you navigate the complex healthcare system, visit: **www.caremanager.org**.

- Learn more about palliative care and what it means here: **wikipedia. org/wiki/Palliative_care**.

- Finding the right Gerontologist for your elder loved ones is critical. Just as you select an OB/GYN specialist when you are pregnant or a pediatrician for a child, a gerontologist specializes in the science of aging and the care of elderly people. To find the right physician for your loved one, here is a web site to help you get started: **www.zocdoc.com**.

- There are a number of medical alert devices on the market that are excellent safety nets should your loved one be alone and need emergency assistance. Here are two resources that can help you start your search: **www.alltimemedical.com/mobility-aids-for-the-elderly. html** and **www.LifeAlertHelp.com**.

10 Tips for Communicating with a Person with Dementia

We aren't born knowing how to communicate with a person with Dementia but we can learn. Improving your communication skills will help make caregiving less stressful and will likely improve the quality of your relationship with your loved one. Good communication skills also will enhance your ability to handle the difficult behavior you may encounter as you care for a person with a dementing illness.

- Set a positive mood for interaction. Your attitude and body language communicate your feelings and thoughts stronger than your words. Set a positive mood by speaking to your loved one in a pleasant and respectful manner.

- Use facial expressions, tone of voice and physical touch to help convey your message and show your feelings of affection.

- Get the person's attention. Limit distractions and noise – turn off the radio or TV, close the curtains or shut the door, or move to quieter surroundings. Before speaking, make sure you have your loved one's attention; address the person by name, identify yourself by name and relation, and use nonverbal cues and touch to help keep the person focused. If seated, be at the same level and maintain eye contact.

- State your message clearly. Use simple words and sentences. Speak slowly, distinctly and in a reassuring tone. Refrain from raising your voice higher or louder; instead, pitch your voice lower. If the person doesn't understand the first time, use the same wording to repeat your message or question. If he or she still doesn't understand, wait a few minutes and rephrase the question. Use the names of people and places instead of pronouns or abbreviations.

- Ask simple, answerable questions. Ask one question at a time; those with yes or no answers work best. Refrain from asking open-ended questions or giving too many choices. For example, ask *"Would you like to wear your white shirt or your blue shirt?"* Better still, show the choices. Visual prompts and cues help clarify your question and can guide the response.

- Listen with your ears, eyes and heart. Be patient in waiting for your loved one's reply. If he or she is struggling for an answer, it's okay to suggest words. Watch for nonverbal cues and body language, and respond appropriately. *Always strive to listen for the meaning and feelings that underlie the words.*

- Break down activities into a series of steps. This makes many tasks much more manageable. You can encourage your loved one to do what he or she can. Gently remind your loved one of the steps if he or she tends to forget and assist with the steps your loved one is no longer able to accomplish alone. Again, visual cues, such as showing with your hand where to place the dinner plate, can be very helpful.

- When the going gets tough, distract and redirect. When your loved one becomes upset, try changing the subject or the environment. For example, ask for help or suggest going for a walk. *It is important to connect with the person on a feeling level, before you redirect.* You might say, *"I see you're feeling sad. I'm sorry you're upset. Let's go get something to eat."*

- Respond with affection and reassurance. People with Dementia often feel confused, anxious and unsure of themselves. Further, they often may recall things that never really occurred. *Avoid trying to correct or convince them they are wrong.* Stay focused on the feelings they are demonstrating (which are real) and respond with verbal and physical expressions of comfort, support and reassurance. Sometimes holding hands, touching, hugging and praise will get the person to respond when all else fails.

- Remember the good old days. Remembering the past is often a soothing and affirming activity. Many people with Dementia may not remember what happened 45 minutes ago, but they can clearly recall their lives 45 years earlier. Therefore, *avoid asking questions that rely on short-term memory,* such as asking the person what they had for lunch. Instead, try asking general questions about the person's distant past. This information is more likely to be retained.

10 Helpful Tips to Prevent Caregiver Burnout

- Soothe yourself with prayer, meditation, repeating positive affirmations or anything else to remind you that you are a wonderful person. It is helpful to join a caregivers' support group.

- Switch your focus: Do something different, change your routine – even if it's just for a few minutes. This will help you return to what you were doing with a fresh perspective.
- Ask for help: Make a list of things you need and concrete ways people can assist you. When people ask what they can do, have them choose from the list.
- Avoid isolation: Spend time with friends, pursue a hobby, take a class and become active in your community.
- Take care of your needs: Eat right, exercise, get enough rest, get regular checkups at the doctor and take time for yourself – spend time alone and/or visit family/friends.
- Express your feelings: Feelings of anger, depression and sadness are common to caregivers. Talk about these feelings with a friend, relative, support group or a therapist.
- Avoid the use of illegal drugs and/or alcohol: These substances do not help to make the situation any better. See a therapist or join a support group to work on issues, instead of ignoring them.
- Remember that you are doing the best that you can. Nobody is perfect or can do everything. Accept assistance if offered and stay positive.
- Consult with trained professionals who have the knowledge and experience with aging issues to help make things easier for you.
- Taking care of yourself first will leave you with the energy needed to be a much more effective caregiver, which is something positive and healthy for your loved one as well.

Things You Should Know About Your Parents' Finances

- **Have your parents named a durable power of attorney to manage their finances?** The first step is to find out if they have named a Durable Power of Attorney (POA). Without a POA in place, you'll have to go to court to get guardianship of your parents in order to access accounts on their behalf.

- **Where do they keep their financial records?** Whether they keep their money and documents in a bank, a safe or under the mattress, you need to know where to find records when you need them. Also find out the location of keys or codes to lock boxes or safes.

- **What are their bank account numbers and names of their financial institutions?** In addition to knowing where they keep their money, you need specifics on all account numbers. What banks and mortgage company do they use? Do they have an investment firm? How many credit card accounts do they have and where do they keep their statements?

- **What are your parents' monthly expenses?** Gather information on their mortgage, car payment, credit card debt, electric bill and other expenses.

- **How do they pay their bills currently?** If there are automatic deductions being taken out of a checking account, you need to know about them. Do they use online banking/bill pay or only paper checks?

- **How much is their annual income and where does it come from?** Do your parents receive monthly pension checks? Do they have dividends coming in from investments? Do they get money for a disability or alimony?

- **Do they receive Medicare, Medicaid or Social Security?** If your parents become incapacitated, you may have to investigate the status and eligibility of government assistance.

- **What kind of medical health insurance do they have in addition to Medicare?** Do they have health insurance provided by an employer? If they are retired, are health benefits included as part of a pension?

- **Do they have long-term-care insurance?** A "regular" health insurance plan does not cover the cost of assisted living or a nursing home. Did they purchase a long-term-care insurance policy to cover the cost of those residences? If not, and they can no longer live on their own, what can they afford in terms of housing?

- **Do they have an accountant or financial planner?** Who is it and how do you contact them? Have they done any estate planning? Ask if you can meet with their financial professional with them to discuss their situation.

5 Important Things Your Loved Ones Should Put in Writing

- Identify the person who will make healthcare decisions for them when they can no longer make their own decisions.
- List all the medications they are taking; both prescription and over the counter.
- Establish your loved ones' feelings regarding hospice and palliative care.
- How do they want people to treat them if they are ill or incapacitated?
- Find out what your loved ones want to know and not know about their care as they grow older.

Top Questions to Ask a Personal Care Home Health Company

Before you select an agency to care for your loved one, ask these questions:

- Does the home care provider supply literature explaining its services, eligibility requirements, fees and funding sources? Many agencies furnish care recipients with a detailed "Patient's Bill of Rights" that outlines the rights and responsibilities of the providers, care recipients and caregivers alike.
- How long has this agency been providing home care services?
- Who owns the home care agency? Is the agency owned by a national corporation or is it locally owned?
- Carefully check any reviews on the agency. You can do a Google search on the company name or go to **www.Caring.com** to find reviews.
- Go to the agency's web site and carefully study it.

- Is the agency licensed by the state?
- What range of home care services does the agency provide?
- Do they offer the specific services you need (e.g., Dementia care, 24-hour live-in care, etc.)?
- Can they meet any special needs you may have (i.e., language or cultural preferences)?
- How does this provider select and train its employees?
- Does it perform regular background checks on staff?
- Does this provider include the client, family members and the patient in developing the Care Plan?
- Is the patient's care documented, detailing the specific tasks to be carried out by each professional caregiver?
- Does the provider assign supervisors to oversee the quality of care that clients are receiving in their homes? If so, how often do these individuals make home visits and spot checks?
- Who can the care recipient and his or her family members call with questions or complaints?
- How does the agency follow up on and resolve problems? This helps ensure that the caregivers are performing the services correctly and responding to the care recipient's changing needs.
- What are the financial procedures of the agency?
- Are caregivers available 24 hours a day, seven days a week? Not all home care agencies are available around the clock or guarantee replacement coverage if the assigned aide is unable to come.

Common Medical Conditions for People Over Age 65

The following are some common conditions that mainly affect seniors. Being aware of these and how to treat and cope with them best are important for caregivers to know. The most widespread condition affecting those 65 and older is heart disease, followed by stroke, cancer, pneumonia and the flu. Accidents, especially falls that result in hip fractures, are also unfortunately common in the elderly. A lot of our elders are coping with at least one of the following conditions, and many are dealing with two or more of the following:

- Heart conditions (hypertension, vascular disease, congestive heart failure, high blood pressure and coronary artery disease)
- Dementia, including Alzheimer's disease
- Depression
- Incontinence (urine and stool)
- Arthritis
- Osteoporosis
- Diabetes
- Breathing problems
- Frequent falls, which can lead to fractures
- Parkinson's disease
- Cancer
- Eye problems (Cataracts, Glaucoma, Macular Degeneration)

As the body ages and changes, other things to be aware of are:

- Slower or delayed reaction time, which is especially important when judging if a person can drive;
- Thinner skin, which can lead to bruises and wounds that don't heal quickly;
- Weakened immune system, which can make fighting off viruses, bacteria and diseases difficult;
- Diminished sense of taste or smell, especially for smokers, which can lead to diminished appetite and dehydration.

Helpful Resources on Medical Conditions that Affect the Elderly

- Parkinson's Disease Association: **www.apdaparkinson.org**
- ALS Association (Lou Gehrig's Disease): **www.als.org**
- Multiple Sclerosis Association: **www.mymsaa.org**
- Alzheimer's Association: **www.alz.org/index.asp**
- Diabetes Association: **www.diabetes.org**
- American Cancer Society: **www.cancer.org**
- American Lung Association: **www.lung.org**

- Geriatric Psychiatry Association: **www.gmhfonline.org/gmhf**
- AARP: **www.aarp.org**

10 Helpful Tips for Taking Medication

A National Institutes of Health study found that 40 percent of seniors age 65 and older take five or more prescription medications, and 90 percent take at least one prescription. The same study found that as many as 55 percent of seniors take their medications incorrectly. Obviously, this is a critical issue in keeping your loved ones safe. Always check with your loved ones' physicians and/or pharmacists regarding any concerns you have about their medications.

- **Storing medications.** Make sure your loved one's medications are kept in a cool dry place and NOT on the window ledge! Keeping medications where sunlight will hit them will vastly weaken the potency of the drug.
- **Taking too much.** Overdoses are the number-one cause of medication fatalities and the most common medication error, according to an FDA study about drug errors. Watch out for loved ones who may be overusing prescription medications. Signs of prescription drug overuse can include: over-sedation, mood swings and running out of medication early.
- **Confusing one medication with another.** Prescription medications frequently have names that are easy to mix up. Examples of medications that are often confused include:
  - Zantac for heartburn and Zyrtec for allergies;
  - Lamictal for epilepsy and Lamisil for fungal infection;
  - Celebrex for arthritis and Celexa for depression
- Patients, particularly seniors with Dementia, also can mix up pills when they look superficially similar. A daily pill-minder can be a big help. Sorting daily medication in advance can prevent the wrong medication from being taken in a moment of confusion.
- **Medicine interactions (and contraindications).** Some medications were never meant to be mixed. With 40 percent of seniors taking five or more prescriptions and many of them receiving these prescriptions from multiple specialists, sometimes patients are

inadvertently prescribed medications or take medications which are dangerous when mixed. Consult with the patient's primary care physician and/or pharmacist to be sure.

- **Food and drug interactions.** While it's common knowledge that certain medications shouldn't be taken at the same time, the issue of foods interacting with drugs is less commonly discussed. For example, many seniors are on medications, such as the anticoagulant Coumadin or blood-thinning statins. Many medicines in this family can be rendered ineffective when a patient eats foods high in vitamin K, such as leafy green vegetables, broccoli and Brussels sprouts. Similarly, grapefruit juice can cause potentially dangerous interactions with at least 85 medications, because it contains a compound that affects the way medications are metabolized by the liver.

- **Wrong route of administration.** The FDA report cited above indicates that 16 percent of medication errors involve using the wrong route of administration. This could involve, for example, swallowing a tablet that was intended to be taken sublingually (slowly absorbed under the tongue) or as an anal suppository (yes, this has happened). Swallowing a liquid intended for injection or use as a nasal spray is another example.

- **Mixing alcohol with medications**. There are plenty of drugs that come with a bright orange warning sticker attached, telling you not to drink alcohol when taking them. However, the sticker can fall off, or not get attached in the first place, or the patient might just really want a cocktail and figure it'll be OK "just this once." But alcohol, combined with a long list of painkillers, sedatives and other medications, becomes a deadly poison in these situations. In fact, many experts now say you shouldn't drink when on *any* medication without first checking with your doctor.

- **Double-dosing by taking a brand-name drug and the generic version at the same time.** With insurance companies mandating the use of generic drugs whenever they're available, it's all too common for patients to get confused and end up with bottles of a brand-name drug and a generic version at the same time without realizing it. For example, a common diuretic is furosemide. The brand name is Lasix. "A patient might have a bottle of furosemide and a bottle of Lasix and not know they're the same thing," says internist Bruce Mann, M.D. "In essence, the patient is taking twice the dose." Since generic drugs don't list the equivalent brand name on the label, you might not spot this unless your brand-name version lists the generic name in the fine print.

- **Taking prescription drugs and over-the-counter or alternative medications without knowing how they interact.** It's easy to think that something you can grab off the shelf at your local grocery or drug store must be safe, but some of the most common OTC drugs can cause serious reactions. A top contender is medicine-chest staple Maalox, meant to calm digestive upset. A new and very popular version, Maalox Total Relief, contains an ingredient called bismuth subsalicylate that can react dangerously with anticlotting drugs, drugs for hypoglycemia and anti-inflammatories, particularly ibuprofen and other nonsteroidal anti-inflammatories. Again, check with your physician and/or pharmacist.

- **Old medications.** Some seniors may stop taking their medications for a period of time for a number of reasons and then start up again. It is important to make sure their medications are not expired.

Proper Nutrition for the Elderly

Getting adequate nutrition can be a challenge as people age, as the number of calories you need begins to decline. Every calorie you consume must be packed with nutrition in order to hit the mark. Several key nutrients, in particular, may be in short supply as you get older. Many nutrients are available in a variety of food choices, however. As with any medication, be sure to consult your physician before taking any supplements. Here are the nine top vitamins and nutrients seniors need and how to get enough:

- **Vitamin B12:** B12 is important for creating red blood cells and DNA, and for maintaining healthy nerve function and energy. Getting enough B12 is a challenge for older people because they can't absorb it from food as well as younger people. **How to hit the mark:** Eat more foods rich in B12, including fish, meat, poultry, eggs, milk and milk products. Talk to your doctor about whether you should take a B12 supplement.

- **Folate/Folic Acid:** You may have heard of folate, as it's often recommended to pregnant and nursing women. Too little of this essential B vitamin is known for contributing to anemia. Older people whose diets don't include a lot of fruits and vegetables or fortified breakfast cereals may be falling short. **How to hit the mark:** If you don't already eat breakfast cereals that are fortified with folate, you might want to start. It's also important to eat plenty of fruits and vegetables. Ask your doctor if you should take a supplement that contains folate.

- **Calcium:** Calcium plays many roles in the body but it is most important for building and maintaining strong bones. Calcium is so essential that if you don't get enough, your body will leach it out of your bones. Coming up short on calcium has been shown to increase the risk of brittle bones and fractures in seniors – a major concern as we all age. **How to hit the mark:** Help yourself to three servings a day of low-fat milk and other dairy products. Other good dietary sources of calcium include kale and broccoli, as well as juices fortified with calcium. Calcium-rich foods are by far the best choice. Smoothies made with yogurt, fruit and even vegetables can be an attractive option for people who have lost their appetite, have trouble chewing or have a dry mouth.

- **Vitamin D:** Vitamin D helps the body absorb calcium, maintain bone density and prevent osteoporosis. Recent findings suggest that vitamin D also may protect against some chronic diseases, including cancer, type 1 diabetes, rheumatoid arthritis, multiple sclerosis and autoimmune diseases. In older people, vitamin D deficiency has also been linked to an increased risk of falling. Many Americans come up short on vitamin D, which is mainly produced by the skin when exposed to sunlight. **How to hit the mark:** Get a little sunshine every day to boost vitamin D (just 10-15 minutes outside each day will help and may also brighten your mood). Many foods are fortified with vitamin D, including cereals, milk, some yogurts and juices. Few foods naturally contain vitamin D. However, vitamin D is found in salmon, tuna and eggs. Researchers are currently debating what the recommended level of vitamin D for optimal health should be. Many experts think older people need to take vitamin D supplements, since the skin becomes less efficient at producing the vitamin from sunlight as we age.

- **Potassium:** Getting enough potassium in our diets may also help keep bones strong. This essential mineral is vital for cell function and has also been shown to help reduce high blood pressure and the risk of kidney stones. Unfortunately, surveys show that many older Americans don't get the recommended 4,700 mg of potassium a day. **How to hit the mark:** Fruits and vegetables are by far the richest dietary sources of potassium. Bananas, prunes, plums and potatoes with their skins are particularly rich in potassium.

- **Magnesium:** Magnesium plays a crucial role in some 300 different physiological processes. Getting enough can help keep your immune system in top shape, your heart healthy and your bones strong. Many whole foods, including vegetables, contain magnesium. **How to hit the mark:** Fill your plate with as many unprocessed foods as possible, including fresh fruits, vegetables, nuts, whole grains, beans and seeds, all of which are great sources of magnesium.

- **Fiber:** Fiber helps promote healthy digestion by moving foods through the digestive tract. Foods rich in fiber, including whole grains, beans, fruits and vegetables, have many other health benefits, including protecting against heart disease. Most Americans only get about half the recommended levels. **How to hit the mark:** Eat more whole grains, nuts, beans, fruits and vegetables every day. Be creative. When you visit your parents, divide up pumpkin seeds, nuts, blueberries or already-chopped vegetables into snack-size bags and leave them in the refrigerator, so they're ready to eat.

- **Omega-3 fats:** These unsaturated (healthy) fats, found primarily in fish, have a wide range of benefits, including possibly reducing symptoms in rheumatoid arthritis and slowing the progression of age-related Macular Degeneration (AMD), a disease of reduced vision in the elderly. Seafood should be part of a heart-healthy diet but omega-3 supplements have not been shown to protect against heart disease. **How to hit the mark:** Nutrition experts recommend helping yourself to at least two servings of fish a week. Salmon, tuna, sardines and mackerel are especially high in omega-3 fats. Some vegetable sources of omega-3 include soybeans, walnuts, flaxseed and canola oil. If you're an adult child trying to help your parents get more omega-3s, I suggest buying canned salmon or tuna to put on salad.

- **Water:** Water might not seem like an essential vitamin or mineral, but it is crucial for good health. With age, the sense of thirst may decline. Certain medicines increase the risk for becoming dehydrated. Water is especially important if you are increasing the fiber in your diet, since it absorbs water. In the modified MyPyramid for older adults, created by Tufts University researchers, eight glasses of fluids a day are next to physical activity in importance for health. **How to hit the mark:** Nutritionists recommend you drink *at least* three to five large glasses of water each day. One sign that you're drinking enough is the color of your urine. It should be pale yellow. If it is bright or dark yellow, you may need to drink more liquids. Adult children can help remind their parents to drink enough water by buying them four-ounce water bottles and encouraging them to drink water often or at least with every snack and meal. Some people may need to have their amount of fluids restricted due to medical reasons, such as kidney or liver disease. Make sure to check with your parents' healthcare provider about a suitable fluid intake level for them.

Mental Health Concerns in Seniors

Did you know that about 20 percent of adults aged 55 or older have experienced some type of mental health concern, but nearly one in three of those seniors do not receive treatment?

Depression and mood disorders also are fairly widespread among older adults, and disturbingly, they often go undiagnosed and untreated. In a 2006 survey by the Centers for Disease Control (CDC) and National Institute of Mental Health, 5 percent of seniors 65 and older reported having current depression, and about 10.5 percent reported a diagnosis of depression at some point in their lives. Caregivers should keep an eye out for the following warning signs, which could indicate a mental health concern:

- Sad or depressed mood lasting longer than two weeks;
- Social withdrawal; loss of interest in things that used to be enjoyable;

- Unexplained fatigue, energy loss or sleep changes;
- Confusion, disorientation, problems with concentration or decision-making;
- Increase or decrease in appetite; changes in weight;
- Memory loss, especially recent or short-term memory problems;
- Feelings of worthlessness, inappropriate guilt, helplessness;
- Thoughts of suicide;
- Physical problems that can't otherwise be explained: aches, constipation, etc.
- Changes in appearance or dress;
- Problems maintaining the home or yard;
- Trouble handling finances or working with numbers.

7 Tips for Long-Distance Caregivers

Being a long-distance caregiver is becoming more and more frequent as the world becomes a smaller place through technology. Yet, some people can feel helpless when living far from a loved one in need. There are some things you can do from a distance to help:

- Understand your loved one's condition, treatments, medications and diet;
- Be conscious of the independence he/she wants/needs;
- Know where important documents are kept;
- Have family and friends nearby check on your loved one if needed;
- Call churches or volunteer groups for meal delivery or transportation;
- Keep a list of important contact numbers, account numbers and even passwords.
- Weigh all the options before moving your loved one out of his/her home. For example, look into a professional personal care home health company.

I hope these resources are helpful for you as you work with your loved ones to enhance their quality of life and safety.

CHAPTER 7

From Russia with Love

I fell in love with Svetlana in 2007 when I went to Moscow to meet her. I'll tell you more about that a bit later. I didn't realize at that time, however, that my relationship with Svetlana would lead me on a wonderful journey experiencing life and love in Russia and Ukraine *and* result in expanded business opportunities. You see, Svetlana is the major reason that I developed *First Home Care*, a home care company in Moscow. I have been fortunate to have visited Russia and Ukraine more than 30 times over the past 15 years.

During my time in Moscow, I realized that the issues of aging, and all the family challenges related to that, are worldwide and not just exclusive to the United States. Pain, suffering and grieving affect us all, no matter what country you live in. This last chapter tells of my journey throughout Eastern Europe and into Asia and the impact it had on me.

As I started my exploration of Russia, I learned so many interesting things. For example, in 1992, a very unusual trend emerged in Russia: There were more deaths than births. The reason for this is not only because of the aging of the Russian population but the de-population that was caused by the profound catastrophic events of the 20th century, including two world wars, the Russian civil war of 1917-1922 and famines in the early 1920s and '30s. These catastrophes have distorted the population pyramid in Russia so much that the typical age distribution and balance between male and female in the population is skewed more toward women. In fact, the huge loss of life during

World War II caused Russia to have the lowest overall male-to-female ratio in the world, especially among the elderly. The irregularities of this pyramid will continue to have an impact on the number of births and the rate of population growth and aging for several decades. This pattern affects such vital spheres as school enrollment, employment, retirement and care of the aging population. It also spawned the international dating industry in Russia and Eastern Europe.

Privet (hello) from Moscow!

As I spent time in Moscow and other places in Eastern Europe, like the Ukraine, I thought that aging here might prove to be easier than in the west, because there remains such a strong emphasis on "the group" over "the individual." Indeed, older adults tend to live with their adult children in Russia. This means that there is not a huge portion of the Russian elderly that are left living alone. However, just because they have support from their families does not mean things are easy for Russian seniors to get what they need. They are extremely disadvantaged when it comes to receiving government support, with limited financial resources designated for them. This puts the main responsibility for the care of the elderly directly on individual families. I found that to be quite ironic, considering their history of communism.

In addition, the population of working men and women is declining steadily. This means that there are fewer people in the workforce earning money to support not only their own families, but their aging parents as well. This is a difficult situation because it appears to have led to a lack of concern for the elderly in Russia. This was a disturbing lesson for me and made me appreciate what we have here in the United States. With all these challenges in Russia, I felt that there was an opportunity to create a niche home healthcare company to help those Russians who had the means to pay for help with caring for an aging loved one.

My venture into home care in Moscow all started with a wonderful love affair with a beautiful Russian woman.

Svetlana

I met Svetlana through an introduction from a couple I became friends with in Orlando, Florida, where I was running a hospice program. My friend Tony met Natalia while visiting Moscow and married her 16 months later. They are a wonderful couple and remain madly in love to this day. One night at dinner, Natalia told me she had a friend in Moscow that she wanted me to meet. I thought to myself, "Sure, what are the chances anything would develop from that?" And then seeing how happy Tony and Natalia were together, I thought, "Why not?!" I remembered an old Russian saying: "Those who do not risk, do not drink the champagne."

Natalia said she would talk to her friend Svetlana to see if she was interested. A week later, Natalia called me and said her friend Svetlana would be interested in learning more about me. Natalia gave me Svetlana's email address and we started a four-month friendship online. We would Skype each other a few times a week. Our friendship grew steadily.

Svetlana was 32, had never been married and was an only-child working as a bank manager in Moscow. This was a prestigious position, especially for a woman in Moscow. She had a great smile, short blond hair and spoke English. Her bubbly personality, positive outlook and adventure for life was contagious.

We agreed to meet and I arranged to visit her over the July Fourth weekend. The anticipation was electrifying as I got ready for my trip to meet Svetlana. I had been to Moscow before, so also looked forward to returning to a city with such a rich history and culture.

My flight left on July 2, connecting through Amsterdam to Moscow. Some people don't like to travel but I am not one of them. The excitement of traveling the world is one of my greatest joys. I am a Million Mile flyer and I hold a Diamond Medallion Platinum status with Delta, so in other words, I really love traveling!

I arrived in Moscow on July 3 at 2:50 p.m. In total, it was a 10-hour flight. Svetlana was waiting for me at the airport. As I came through Passport Control and Customs, I saw Svetlana's beautiful smiling face. My heart was beating 1,000 miles a minute. We shared a big hug and modest kiss and we were off and running. We took a cab to the Marriott Grand Hotel where I stayed. The hotel is in the heart of Moscow, about a 20-minute walk from the Kremlin and near the Pushkin Metro station. Moscow has an elaborate subway system, which carries about 8 million people per day. Each Metro station is a piece of art and reflects a part of Russian history.

Svetlana and I at the Pushkin Café in Moscow

I remember every detail of our first encounter like it was yesterday. I checked in and we had a glass of wine in the hotel bar. One thing I loved about Svetlana is the way she talks. Our conversations were always engaging and fun. We spent a few hours laughing and getting to know each other in person. While I had just met her face to face, my feelings for her were growing by the minute. I had made dinner reservations for that evening at the Pushkin Café, a five-star restaurant in Moscow – one of my favorite places to eat when I'm in the city. Pushkin Café has three levels to it and we had a wonderful table on the second level known as "the Library." We started our wonderful dinner with a bottle of Champagne. I truly felt like I was in the movie, *Dr. Zhivago*. We enjoyed a very traditional Russian dinner and it was a wonderful first date that I will remember forever. For an appetizer, we ate herring mixed with boiled potatoes, beets, carrots and mayonnaise. We both had a fish soup with carrot, spices and potato. For our main course, I had a whole sea bass, while Svetlana had a meat dish called *Otbivnaya,* which is a combination of beef and pork. We also shared a dish called *Syrniki* – a cottage cheese cutlet. Dessert was a wonderful pastry dish made with apples.

During our five days together, we visited some wonderful places in Moscow, including Red Square and the Kremlin, took a boat ride on the Moscow River and enjoyed several wonderful restaurants and museums. One afternoon, we had a picnic in a park next to the Kremlin. Taking in the atmosphere of Moscow with Svetlana was like being in a dream.

During the following months, we visited Paris, Spain and Jamaica together, as our love grew. Yes, we were in love. It was during one of my visits back to Moscow to see her where the seeds to my business venture into home care took root.

Getting the Business Started in Moscow

During one of my visits to see Svetlana in Moscow, I met my future business partner, which led to the start of my first home care business in Russia. A few days before I was to leave for a visit with Svetlana in May, she called me and asked if I would bring a suit with me to wear to a special dinner her bank was holding for their major clients at the Pushkin Café. I was excited to attend the event and see Svetlana in action, as well as to eat at my favorite restaurant again.

The bank had reserved the whole second floor at the Pushkin Café. There were about 50 people in attendance. Svetlana looked glorious in a black backless dress and high heels. Her blond hair radiated along with her smile. If I do say so myself, we made a great looking couple.

During the evening, I met a gentleman named Alexander who was the CEO of a company called MediCapital One, a medical development company. I hit it off with Alexander, as he spoke English well and his mother and brother lived in Philadelphia. We discussed healthcare, as that was a common interest for both of us. It was a wonderful evening and I was so proud of Svetlana, as I watched her work the room and interact with her customers. Before the evening ended, Alexander and I shared business cards.

Two weeks later while back home, I received a call from Alexander. He told me his company was getting ready to build a hospital in an up-and-coming part of Moscow called New Riga. Alexander asked if I would be interested in consulting with his company on the concept designs for the hospital, as he wished to integrate some American ideas. Because I had 16 years of experience working in hospitals, I was honored he asked me. We drew up a contract and I visited Moscow three times over the next eight months on this consulting project. During my first visit, I met Alexander's company's chief operating officer, a woman named Vika. As I spent time with Alexander and Vika, we shared stories about healthcare, and in particular home care. I told them of my *Homewatch CareGivers* operation, which intrigued them. We agreed to formally study the idea and see where it would lead us.

Throughout this time, as I consulted on the project for Alexander and considered the possibility of opening a home care company in Moscow, I was so happy to have a woman like Svetlana in my life. It was during one of my visits to Moscow that I asked Svetlana to come to the United States, so we could start a real life together. Up to this point, every time we met was like a honeymoon, and while I loved this romantic affair, I wanted more. Much to my surprise, Svetlana declined my offer saying that she did not want to give up her life in Moscow. I was crushed. I told her I would split my time between Plymouth, Michigan, where I lived, and Moscow. She turned down this idea, too, and I had to accept the hard fact that my love for Svetlana was greater than her love for me. We discontinued our romantic relationship. After several months of mending my broken heart, we still maintained a friendship and she was instrumental in helping me navigate the Russian business and legal system, as I started my first home care company in that country.

Moving Forward

On a subsequent visit to Moscow, I met a woman named Elena. She was a professor at Moscow University. She asked me to give a lecture to her business and marketing class. I was honored to be asked, so I spoke to her class about U.S. healthcare and the marketing of healthcare services. The graduate level class had 18 students, who all spoke English. I told the students I was considering opening a home care company in Moscow, which led to an interesting dialogue about doing business in Russia. I had a great time, as did the students. I learned as much from them as they did from me.

I developed a lasting friendship with Elena, who also was helpful as I explored the feasibility of a home care company in Moscow. During one of our Skype sessions, Elena told me her students wanted to do their class project on my idea of opening a home care company. I was intrigued, as I did need to complete an environmental assessment to get a better feel for the market, as well as the potential demand and any competition. Elena and I agreed that on my next trip, we would hold a class on what needs to go into an environmental assessment. Alexander and Vika also were excited about the prospect of hearing what the students came up with.

My friend Elena's grad school class assisted me with my environmental assessment in Moscow.

During my next trip, I spent half of a Saturday with the students going over our approach. I was pleasantly surprised at how resourceful the students were with their ideas. The students spent the next month conducting their research and here is what they found: To my surprise, there were 12 home health companies currently functioning in Moscow. This told me that there was a real need. Also, while the number of competitors was small relative to the Moscow population of 11.5 million, it still demonstrated people are using home care services. I also found out there are over 60 hospitals and clinics in Moscow. Interestingly, after World War II, the Russians over-built their hospital system in anticipation of a third World War. In the heart of Moscow, there are eight privately held large hospitals. This was also a good sign, as the researchers and I all felt we could develop some productive strategic partnerships.

The constitution of the Russian Federation provides all citizens the right to free healthcare under mandatory medical insurance. This healthcare is not the best, to say the least. So, if you are a Russian in need of healthcare, you enter the Russian healthcare system and hope for the best or you pay for a private experience. One privately owned hospital in particular was a big sign to me that the Russian people would spend the money for quality healthcare. This specialty hospital is dedicated to providing a total pre-natal, delivery and post-natal experience for mothers. The private obstetrics hospital offered a package for $35,000 that included all your care before, during and after pregnancy. They have a waiting list for their services, so this showed us that the Russian people were willing and able to spend money for quality healthcare services.

Alexander, Vika and I reviewed the environmental assessment completed by the students and agreed to move to the next step and write a business plan. I spent the next few weeks writing one. With the approval of the business plan, we moved into implementation.

My business partner Alexander and I in Moscow discussing First Home Care

The Birth of *First Home Care*

We formally started *First Home Care* (**www.first-homecare.com**) in July 2009. The business was structured where MediCapital One owned 51 percent of the business, and I owned 49 percent. Svetlana was helpful in finding me an attorney in Moscow to help me put together our agreement.

We hired Olga, our executive director, a scheduler named Alfia and a sales person named Anton. MediCapital One gave us an office to work out of as well as access to their legal team and Human Resources staff. It was a nice set up. Part of my contribution was flying Olga and Alfia over to *Homewatch CareGivers'* headquarters in Plymouth, Michigan, where they spent two weeks going through a training and orientation program at my personal home care agency and several other skilled home care agencies. *First Home Care* offers a combination of skilled and personal home care services. Olga and Alfia learned a tremendous amount about the home care business in the United States and we had a productive visit.

Another part of my arrangement with the business was to provide on-site training. To start, I sent my assistant Melissa to Moscow. She went over in February 2010. To this date, she still hates me for sending her there in the heart of a Russian winter. Melissa's visit, however, was immensely successful in helping *First Home Care* get up and running.

Since 2010, I have flown to Moscow several times a year to help with business development efforts. I've had a wonderful time doing business in Russia. This was a great experience and I am very proud to say I own a home healthcare company in Moscow!

The business has grown and we have developed several strategic partnerships with hospitals and hospices located in Moscow.

Exploring Ukraine

One of the wonderful things that came out of my venture in Moscow was the discovery of Ukraine, a country that borders Russia to the east and northeast. It was part of the Soviet republic but became independent in 1991. On one of my visits to Moscow, I flew down to Kiev and just fell in love with the city. Kiev is the capital and largest city of Ukraine, located in the north central part of the country on the Dnieper River. The city truly is a jewel, and I found the history, culture, food and beautiful women of Ukraine simply amazing. Kiev is home to about 2.8 million people, making it the eighth largest city in Europe. I found a wonderful hotel named the Premier Palace that became my home base on subsequent visits.

Kiev is an important industrial, scientific, educational and cultural center of Eastern Europe, featuring many high-tech industries, higher education institutions and world-famous historical landmarks. The city has an extensive infrastructure and a highly developed system of public transportation, including the Kiev Metro. I would recommend visiting Kiev if you ever get the chance.

The city's name is said to derive from the name of Kyi, one of the four legendary founders of Kiev. It remains one of the oldest cities in Eastern Europe, and has passed through several stages of great prominence and relative obscurity over the past 1,500 years. The city probably existed as a commercial center as early as the fifth century. A Slavic settlement on the great trade route between Scandinavia and Constantinople, Kiev was nearly completely destroyed during the Mongol invasion of 1240, losing most of its influence for centuries to come. At other points in history, Kiev was a provincial capital of marginal importance in the outskirts of the territories controlled by its powerful neighbors; first the Grand Duchy of Lithuania, followed by Poland and then Russia. As you can tell, I love history! That's probably more history than you wanted to hear, but it demonstrates the richness of Kiev.

On one of my trips there, I decided to fly down to Sevastopol in the Crimea, a semi-autonomous region of Ukraine about an hour's flight from the capital. I fell in love with this seaport on the Black Sea. Sevastopol has a population of over 342,000, with most of the residents concentrated near the Bay of Sevastopol and surrounding areas. The location and navigability of the city's harbors have made Sevastopol a strategically important port and naval base throughout history. Sevastopol also is home to the Russian Black Sea Fleet, which is why it has significant military importance (and probably the main reason why Russia's President Vladimir Putin was interested in annexing the Crimea in 2014 and invading this beautiful city).

Although relatively small at 334 square miles, Sevastopol's unique naval and maritime features provide the basis for a varied and vibrant economy. The city enjoys mild winters and moderately warm summers; characteristics that help make it a popular seaside resort and tourist destination, mainly for visitors from the former Soviet republic and other Eastern European countries. The city also is an important center for marine biology; in particular, researchers have studied and trained dolphins in the city since the end of World War II. Sevastopol is a walking museum. It was settled by the Greeks in ancient times, so the city has a long, storied past.

While in Sevastopol, I met Kamila. After Svetlana, I thought I would never find another woman I could love. I embarked on a whirlwind romance with Kamila, dating on and off over a three-year period. Kamila helped me appreciate and understand the Ukrainian culture. Unfortunately, my relationship with Kamila did not develop further but we remain wonderful friends to this day.

When I was in Moscow and Ukraine, I thought a great deal about my father, who had a little Russian blood in him. I am sure he was smiling down upon me as I experienced and enjoyed the Russian and Ukrainian cultures. I'm also sure he would have approved of both Svetlana and Kamila.

Kamila in Sevastopol – a beautiful city on the Black Sea in the Crimean Peninsula

While in Ukraine, I studied their healthcare system. Oh boy, what a mess! I don't wish to be disrespectful, but it's hard to see how such a wonderful country could have such a sub-par healthcare system. As I came to love Ukraine, I became interested in their hospice and palliative care movement. I was asked to consult on end-of-life issues in Ukraine by the Ukrainian Federation of Palliative Care. All these experiences further solidify how blessed we are in the United States to have the health system we do.

Ukraine's Struggles for Palliative Care and Hospice

The conflict in Ukraine caused by the Russian invasion of Crimea not only changed the political landscape, it hampered efforts to advance Ukraine's efforts to give their people a better health system, including the development of hospice and palliative care services.

Kseniya Shapoval is the International Palliative Care Initiative Coordinator for the Public Health Program of the International Renaissance Foundation in Ukraine. She writes about the advocacy involved in dealing with palliative care as a *human right* in Ukraine. It was interesting to me that hospice and palliative care was viewed as a human rights issue. Kseniya provided me with a brief overview detailing some challenges and her views on palliative medicine. I wanted to share some of it with you. Again, it helps me appreciate all we have here in this country.

In 2009, oral morphine in Ukraine was not available. There were neither human rights organizations nor strong associations involved in protecting the rights of palliative care patients or defending the interests of physicians. This is such a big contrast from what we have in the United States.

Up to 2009, the Ukrainian Ministry of Health had not implemented any programs concerning the development of palliative care. Moreover, when a senior researcher with Human Rights Watch (HRW) asked one of the officials of the Ministry of Health about the limited use of morphine, the reply was that no complaints on this issue had been received. This demonstrated how out of touch the government was with people's needs!

But in Ukraine, there was pain. This pain claimed many names, faces, lives and families. There were people dying in agony, left to be cared for by their families without any opportunity to get adequate pain relief.

Each year, more than 80,000 people die from cancer in Ukraine – most of them dying in pain! If cancer patients, who require analgesia with morphine or other opioids, aren't able to access medicine, then it is not likely that patients with diseases other than cancer are receiving adequate pain relief either.

In May 2011, a report entitled, "Uncontrolled Pain: Ukraine's Obligation to Ensure Evidence-Based Palliative Care," was submitted to the government of Ukraine. The main story in the report was about Vlad Zhukovsky, a young man from Cherkasy. The report detailed Vlad's heroic yet painful death from cancer and became known around the world.

A large-scale information campaign entitled, "Stop Pain," was held in 2012-2013 in Ukraine, and the provision of legal aid was organized in Rivne, Kharkiv and the Crimea (Sevastopol) areas. In 2013, Ukrainian human rights organizations that had been formed to monitor the provision of pain relief and palliative care to patients prepared a report entitled, "We Have the Right to Live Without Pain and Suffering."

In February 2013, Ukrainian companies were registered to begin producing tablet morphine, and in March, the first deliveries were made to all pharmacies in the country. April of that year saw changes to the Ministry of Health order allowing prescriptions of controlled medicines for pain relief. At last, real changes began happening for the good of patients in Ukraine!

In May, the Cabinet of Ministers of Ukraine approved a resolution on drug trafficking in the medical sphere, which seriously altered the system of care provisions to patients at home by creating opportunities to store opioids for up to 15 days. Previously, a commission of three doctors had to prescribe opioids and patients were not allowed to keep medications at home.

The country had made some progress but there was still much to accomplish. The main issue on developing the practical application of new rules and regulations for using morphine to help control pain was not yet in place. One case serves as a vivid example of this. The Bucha Case, as it was known, is one of a number of high-profile cases that were under investigation with the assistance of the ombudsman in Ukraine.

Ms. Shapoval shared a heart-felt story that took place in Bucha, which is a small town on the outskirts of Kiev. Bucha was the home of a woman named Lyudmyla, who was ill with cancer and home-bound. Doctors prescribed her morphine because of severe pain in March 2012.

It wasn't until January 1, 2013, that Lyudmyla successfully was approved to receive some morphine ampoules to manage her pain (40 ml per night). She had been in pain for nine months! This story shows how fortunate we are in the United States. No patient would ever go that long in pain in this country.

According to the regulations at the time, the function of providing pain relief to these patients could only be carried out by local clinics. Also, morphine had to be delivered by ambulance, but in January 2013, ambulances in Ukraine were forbidden to carry controlled drugs to chronically ill patients. Sadly, Lyudmyla died on March 21, 2013, without the morphine ever having reached her. She died in agony without the ability to demand her right to death without pain.

The story of Lyudmyla and her dire situation spread from human rights organizations, the Ukrainian League for Hospice and Palliative Care

Development and the Office of the Commissioner for Human Rights to all levels of the Ministry of Health.

Kseniya went on to write, "We engaged everyone in solving the problem – the State Service of Ukraine on Drug Control, the Ministry of Interior, doctors of palliative service and the press. But the negotiations had no outcome – the patient did not receive the long-awaited prescription for morphine."

This case is very revealing how politics and the healthcare system's lack of focus on the patient contributes to pain and suffering. While some progress has been made in Ukraine, the fact remains that people are still dying in needless pain. As of the printing of this book, the gift of hospice and palliative care is still not available in Ukraine.

I love Ukraine and will always have a special place in my heart for the country, the people and their culture and history. Despite all of Ukraine's healthcare issues and challenges, I'm more determined than ever to see what I can do to help improve the care people receive in this beautiful country. Unfortunately, the economy and volatile political situation make it impossible to offer a sustainable home healthcare company like I have in Moscow. This is disheartening because as the population continues to age and the need to care for people will increase, I believe their needs will go unattended.

Where Do I Go From Here?

I'm sure my mother and father never would have imagined when I graduated from nursing school at Mercy College in Detroit that my journey in healthcare would have led me to where I am today. I can't believe it myself sometimes. I am truly blessed that my career in healthcare helped me prepare for the work I'm doing today. As I've spoken about it throughout the book, the true impetus for my venture into home care were my experiences of caring for my mother and father, as they aged and passed away. The lessons I learned and shared in this book have allowed me to help thousands of families care for their aging loved ones in a better, less stressful way.

In the United States, my *Homewatch CareGivers* company in Plymouth, Michigan, is proud to be a community resource that provides experienced, loving caregivers to families in need, as well as valuable information and assistance navigating the local, state and national healthcare systems. *First Home*

Care in Moscow, Russia, continues to grow and we are currently looking to partner with one of the privately run hospitals in Moscow to strengthen our infrastructure and grow to serve even more people. The current political environment and economic pressure in Russia make conducting business challenging but we're forging ahead.

As I write this book, I am exploring the development of home care companies in Thailand, Singapore, Vietnam and China with several different partners. The need for home care and the changes in how families care for aging loved ones make these ventures possible. Asia is not only an emerging economic power but a region open to better ways to deal with the aging of their population. In my visits to China, Vietnam and Thailand, I have found newly developing healthcare systems, born out of the issues related to aging, where caring for the aging population is starting to consume a tremendous amount of resources.

To address these aging challenges, for example, the Singapore government offers grants for the training of caregivers. In Vietnam, there are many private hospitals being built and the state of healthcare in general is changing. As the Chinese population continues to age, both the public and private sectors will need to work together to develop solutions that bring cost-effective healthcare to the elderly. Thus far, the central government has publicly stated its policy, commonly referred to as the "90/7/3" framework. This policy means the Chinese government wants to see 90 percent of all seniors receive the care they need in their homes with 7 percent through community hospitals and 3 percent through nursing homes. As of today, the supporting policies that will clearly signal to private investors what exactly to make of the 90/7/3 policy have not fully emerged. This is one of the reasons China is so attractive to me. Time will tell if all this translates into the ability to develop a viable home care business in China.

As I come to the end of the tale of my personal journey, my wish for you is that this book has been a helpful resource, giving you useful and better ways of caring for your aging loved ones. Through my experiences, stories and hard lessons learned on my life's journey, I hope I was able to make a difference in *your* life.

For more information about how you can make the most of your life's journey in taking care of your loved ones, please visit **www.asonsjourney. com**. Through the website, you'll be able to contact me and let me know how you are doing, to ask any questions about personal home care or to seek a helpful hand as you embark on your journey.

Here's to a long and healthy life for you and your loved ones!

Resources

Caregivers

- *Homewatch CareGivers*: **www.homewatchcaregivers.com**
- CareInHomes: **www.careinhomes.com**
- A Place for Mom: **www.aplaceformom.com**
- Caring.Com: **www.caring.com**

Dementia and Alzheimer's Disease

- The National Institutes of Health, National Institute on Aging site, on Alzheimer's disease and vascular Dementia for caregivers: **www.nia.nih.gov/Alzheimers/default.htm**
- Vascular Dementia fact sheet from the National Institutes of Health: **www.nia.nih.gov/Alzheimers/Publications/Dementia.htm**
- The Alzheimer's Society in Great Britain: **www.alzheimers.org.uk/**
- The Merck manual of Geriatrics: **www.merck.com**
- CareFinderPros: **www.carefinderpros.com; Dr.Mike@carefinder-pros.com**

Fall Prevention

- *Homewatch CareGivers **Fall Prevention Guide***: **www.businesswire.com/news/home/20130918005975/en/Homewatch-CareGivers-releases-falls-prevention-guide-living#.VM605-85DIU**
- Fall Prevention Resource Guide: **www.tompkins-co.org/cofa/Services/documents/2013-March30FallPreventionResourceGuide-onlinerevisiononly.pdf**
- Fall Prevention Tips: **www.activeforever.com/fall-prevention**

Hospice

- National Hospice and Palliative Care Organization: **www.nhpco.org**
- Hospice Net: **hospicenet.org**
- Hospice and Palliative Care Center: **hospicecarecenter.org/content/resources**
- International Association for Hospice and Palliative Care: **www.hospicecare.com/resources**
- Hospice Foundation of America: **hospicefoundation.org**
- Seasons Hospice and Palliative Care: **www.seasons.org**

About the Author: Kurt Kazanowski

Kurt Kazanowski is an author, speaker, coach and consultant in the areas of aging, hospice and home care. He is a native of Detroit, Michigan, and has over three decades of experience in the field of healthcare. He received his bachelor's degree in nursing from Mercy College of Detroit and practiced as a public health nurse for many years. Today, Kurt is the owner of two successful personal care home health companies – *Homewatch CareGivers* in Michigan, where he lives, and *First Home Care* in Moscow, Russia.

As a nurse, healthcare executive, author, speaker and successful entrepreneur, Kurt has written numerous articles to help people meet the challenges related to aging, illness and end-of-life care. His most recent book, ***A Son's Journey: Taking Care of Mom and Dad***, is about Kurt's personal journey taking care of his aging parents.

Kurt helps healthcare organizations develop the necessary strategies to improve service delivery, grow market share and enhance profitability. Kurt's authority on the subject of aging and the care of elderly loved ones stems from his work as a nurse, his executive leadership in hospitals, home care and hospice companies, and as the owner of two home health companies. Through his tireless devotion to providing expert care, he has helped thousands of families care for their loved ones.

In his 30 years as a healthcare business executive, Kurt has acquired a specific set of skills and competencies in creating and executing mission and business objectives, strategy development, marketing, sales, referrals, and growth and business development tactics. He also specializes in merger and acquisitions, physician relations, forming strategic partnerships between hospices and hospitals and is an authority in functioning as a connector, facilitator and networker. Kurt's capacity for assisting people and organizations addresses the challenges of aging, as end-of-life care issues span from one family to large complex health systems.

Kurt speaks nationally *and* internationally, as he values the ability to share his knowledge and experiences as both a loving son and a professional in assisting hospice providers, home care companies and hospitals develop new business strategies to care for our increasingly aging population better and more effectively.

For more information about Kurt or to engage him as a speaker for your next group or association meeting, visit **www.kurtkazanowski.com** or email him at **kaznow@comcast.net**.

Praise for

A Son's Journey:
Taking Care of Mom and Dad

"This is a beautifully written and compelling story about the impact of aging family members. We all have faced or will face these types of decisions. Understanding that there are resources and services that help to not only provide guidance and support but make the transition easier benefits everyone. The story being told from a personal point of view explaining the challenges and the benefits of services available makes the issues more personal and understandable for people who are faced with decisions about their loved ones. I would recommend this book to all family members." – **Debra A. Geihsler, Principal, Activate Healthcare, Chicago, Illinois**

"As a home care owner myself, I can honestly say that this book was spot-on accurate. It was incredibly well-researched, informative and kept my interest. The way the author was able to interweave the story of his parents with helpful advice was nothing short of brilliant. I found the book to be a fantastic read while being both entertaining and informative. It is clear that the author is an expert in his field, and sharing his knowledge with his readers is a true gift. I've read a number of books about home care and caregiving, but this one clearly stands at the top of my list." – **Jon Hersh, President, Homewatch CareGivers, Columbus, Ohio**

"What a wonderful read! Kurt does an excellent job of providing critical information and resources to aid in the difficult situation of elder parent care. His ability to weave in personal experiences and provide a compassionate perspective for the caregiver makes you feel like he's a good friend who knows exactly what you are going through ... and he does! As someone just beginning this journey with their parents, I found the information in this book invaluable. Understanding options, signs of caregiver burnout and resources available to me will allow the transition to go more smoothly and hopefully alleviate some of the guilt I'm sure I will experience. I have recommended this book to many friends finding themselves in the predicament of being a caregiver to their loved ones. I also believe my parents will gain much by reading this book and understanding what they may experience, as well as understanding my siblings' and my perspectives. I truly enjoyed getting to know Kurt from his stories and learning about the history of palliative healthcare. And I have even more of an appreciation of the advantages I enjoy, living in this tremendous nation. I'm sure everyone will benefit from the wealth of information provided and find the presentation enjoyable and easy to read." – **Angela P. Colarusso, Health Physicist, PMP, STSM, Las Vegas, Nevada**

"As a Board Certified Physician in Geriatrics and Hospice and Palliative Care and a physician who cares for homebound elderly patients, I found this book a must-read for adult children caring for a loved one. Many of the topics that Kurt addresses I find universal in caring for the very aged population. Many of the children of my patients are facing the challenges Kurt outlines and he provides sage advice on ways to manage difficult situations. *A Son's Journey* provides a wealth of information and the stories told are very heartfelt and inspiring. I especially liked the chapter on the Gift of Hospice as it demystifies hospice and shows how hospice care truly is a gift to be offered. I also liked the chapter on how to talk to aging parents about difficult but necessary topics. This book was enjoyable to read and relevant. I encourage anyone who is caring for an aging loved one to consider this an excellent reference." – **Elizabeth Morgan, M.D., Albuquerque, New Mexico**

Book Kurt to Speak at Your Next Event or Meeting Today!

Many people struggle with juggling their own lives – taking care of their children while trying to help parents age safely with grace and dignity. A challenge to say the least! Kurt's heartfelt presentation will help you learn how to deal with these challenges. Through the sharing of his real-life experiences of love, loss and caring, your group will learn valuable life lessons. Kurt's stories of caring for his aging parents and their eventual deaths and how he managed their end-of-life care will provide useful information, helpful tips and resources that will make your journey with your loved ones smoother, happier and more constructive.

Kurt's authority on the challenges of caring for aging loved ones comes from his three decades of experience in healthcare, starting as a nurse, then as a hospital executive and finally as a senior leader of several home care and hospice organizations. These experiences were enriched by Kurt's ownership of a personal care home health company called *Homewatch CareGivers*, which, over the years, has helped thousands of families care for their loved ones.

Kurt is a visionary whose inspiration and passion is contagious. A dynamic speaker, Kurt's programs get audiences actively thinking about how to make a difference in their parents' lives as they age, as well as their own.

To book Kurt for your next event or meeting, please call him directly at **734.658.6162** or email him at **kaznow@comcast.net**.

For more information about *A Son's Journey: Taking Care of Mom and Dad*, visit the website at **www.asonsjourney.com**.

Share ***A Son's Journey: Taking Care of Mom and Dad*** with your loved ones, friends and colleagues today.

To order more copies of ***A Son's Journey***, please visit **www.asonsjourney.com** or purchase the book directly on Amazon.

CPSIA information can be obtained at www.ICGtesting.com
Printed in the USA
BVOW06s1914051215

429438BV00027B/317/P